Plato — Five Dialogues:
Euthyphro, Apology, Crito, Meno, Phaedo

by

Plato

www.books.com.co

Published by LG Classics
Copyright © 2016 by LG Classics
Cover Copyright © 2016 by LG Classics
All rights reserved.

First Printing March 2016
Printed in the United States of America.
10 9 8 7 6 5 4 3 2 1

LG Classics
New York, New York
www.books.com.co

TABLE OF CONTENTS

I.

Euthyphro

PERSONS OF THE DIALOGUE:

SOCRATES;

EUTHYPHRO

4 Plato

Scene: The Porch of the King Archon

Euthyphro. Why have you left the Lyceum, Socrates? and what are you doing in the Porch of the King Archon? Surely you cannot be concerned in a suit before the King, like myself?

Socrates. Not in a suit, Euthyphro; impeachment is the word which the Athenians use.

Euth. What! I suppose that some one has been prosecuting you, for I cannot believe that you are the prosecutor of another.

Soc. Certainly not.

Euth. Then some one else has been prosecuting you?

Soc. Yes.

Euth. And who is he?

Soc. A young man who is little known, Euthyphro; and I hardly know him: his name is Meletus, and he is of the deme of Pitthis. Perhaps you may remember his appearance; he has a beak, and long straight hair, and a beard which is ill grown.

Euth. No, I do not remember him, Socrates. But what is the charge which he brings against you?

Soc. What is the charge? Well, a very serious charge, which shows a good deal of character in the young man, and for which he is certainly not to be despised. He says he knows how the youth are corrupted and who are their corruptors. I fancy that he must be a wise man, and seeing that I am the reverse of a wise man, he has found me out, and is going to accuse me of corrupting his young friends. And of this our mother the state is to be the judge. Of all our political men he is the only one who seems to me to begin in the right way, with the cultivation of virtue in youth; like a good husbandman, he makes the young shoots his first care, and clears away us who are the destroyers of them. This is only the first step; he will afterwards attend to the elder branches; and if he goes on as he has begun, he will be a very great public benefactor.

Euth. I hope that he may; but I rather fear, Socrates, that the opposite will turn out to be the truth. My opinion is that in attacking you he is simply aiming a blow at the foundation of the state. But in what way does he say that you corrupt the young?

Soc. He brings a wonderful accusation against me, which at first hearing excites surprise: he says that I am a poet or maker of gods, and that I invent new gods and deny the existence of old ones; this is the ground of his indictment.

Euth. I understand, Socrates; he means to attack you about the familiar sign which occasionally, as you say, comes to you. He thinks that you are a neologian, and he is going to have you up before the court for this. He knows that such a charge is readily received by the world, as I myself know too well; for when I speak in the assembly about divine things, and foretell the future to them, they laugh at me and think me a madman. Yet every word that I say is true. But they are jealous of us all; and we must be brave and go at them.

Soc. Their laughter, friend Euthyphro, is not a matter of much consequence. For a man may be thought wise; but the Athenians, I suspect, do not much trouble themselves about him until he begins to impart his wisdom to others, and then for some reason or other, perhaps, as you say, from jealousy, they are angry.

Euth. I am never likely to try their temper in this way.

Soc. I dare say not, for you are reserved in your behaviour, and seldom impart your wisdom. But I have a benevolent habit of pouring out myself to everybody, and would even pay for a listener, and I am afraid that the Athenians may think me too talkative. Now if, as I was saying, they would only laugh at me, as you say that they laugh at you, the time might pass gaily enough in the court; but perhaps they may be in earnest, and then what the end will be you soothsayers only can predict.

Euth. I dare say that the affair will end in nothing, Socrates, and that you will win your cause; and I think that I shall win my own.

Soc. And what is your suit, Euthyphro? are you the pursuer or the defendant?

Euth. I am the pursuer.

Soc. Of whom?

Euth. You will think me mad when I tell you.

Soc. Why, has the fugitive wings?

Euth. Nay, he is not very volatile at his time of life.

Soc. Who is he?

Euth. My father.

Soc. Your father! my good man?

Euth. Yes.

Soc. And of what is he accused?

Euth. Of murder, Socrates.

Soc. By the powers, Euthyphro! how little does the common herd know of the nature of right and truth. A man must be an extraordinary man, and have made great strides in wisdom, before he could have seen his way to bring such an action.

Euth. Indeed, Socrates, he must.

Soc. I suppose that the man whom your father murdered was one of your relatives-clearly he was; for if he had been a stranger you would never have thought of prosecuting him.

Euth. I am amused, Socrates, at your making a distinction between one who is a relation and one who is not a relation; for surely the pollution is the same in either case, if you knowingly associate with the murderer when you ought to clear yourself and him by proceeding against him. The real question is whether the murdered man has been justly slain. If justly, then your duty is to let the matter alone; but if unjustly, then even if the murderer lives under the same roof with you and eats at the same table, proceed against him. Now the man who is dead was a poor dependent of mine who worked for us as a field labourer on our farm in Naxos, and one day in a fit of drunken passion he got into a quarrel with one of our domestic servants and slew him. My father bound him hand and foot and threw him into a ditch, and then sent to Athens to ask of a diviner what he should do with him. Meanwhile he never attended to him and took no care about him, for he regarded him as a murderer; and thought that no great harm would be done even if he did die. Now this was just what happened. For such was the effect of cold and hunger and chains upon him, that before the messenger returned from the diviner, he was dead. And my father and family are angry with me for taking the part of the murderer and prosecuting my father. They say that he did not kill him, and that if he did, dead man was but a murderer, and I ought not to take any notice, for that a son is impious who prosecutes a father. Which shows, Socrates, how little they know what the gods think about piety and impiety.

Soc. Good heavens, Euthyphro! and is your knowledge of religion and of things pious and impious so very exact, that, supposing the circumstances to be as you state them, you are not afraid lest you too may be doing an impious thing in bringing an action against your father?

Euth. The best of Euthyphro, and that which distinguishes him, Socrates, from other men, is his exact knowledge of all such matters. What should I be good for without it?

Soc. Rare friend! I think that I cannot do better than be your disciple. Then before the trial with Meletus comes on I shall challenge him, and say that I have always had a great interest in religious questions, and now, as he charges me with rash imaginations and innovations in religion, I have become your disciple. You, Meletus, as I shall say to him, acknowledge Euthyphro to be a great theologian, and sound in his opinions; and if you approve of him you ought to approve of me, and not have me into court; but if you disapprove, you should begin by indicting him who is my teacher, and who will be the ruin, not of the young, but of the old; that is to say, of myself whom he instructs, and of his old father whom he admonishes and chastises. And if Meletus refuses to listen to me, but will go on, and will not shift the indictment from me to you, I cannot do better than repeat this challenge in the court.

Euth. Yes, indeed, Socrates; and if he attempts to indict me I am mistaken if I do not find a flaw in him; the court shall have a great deal more to say to him than to me.

Soc. And I, my dear friend, knowing this, am desirous of becoming your disciple. For I observe that no one appears to notice you- not even this Meletus; but his sharp eyes have found me out at once, and he has indicted me for impiety. And therefore, I adjure you to tell me the nature of piety and impiety, which you said that you knew so well, and of murder, and of other offences against the gods. What are they? Is not piety in every action always the same? and impiety, again- is it not always the opposite of piety, and also the same with itself, having, as impiety, one notion which includes whatever is impious?

Euth. To be sure, Socrates.

Soc. And what is piety, and what is impiety?

Euth. Piety is doing as I am doing; that is to say, prosecuting any one who is guilty of murder, sacrilege, or of any similar crime-whether he be your father or mother, or whoever he may be-that makes no difference; and not to prosecute them is impiety. And please to consider, Socrates, what a notable proof I will give you of the truth of my words, a proof which I have already given to others:-of the principle, I mean, that the impious, whoever he may be, ought not to go unpunished. For do not men regard Zeus as the best and most righteous of the gods?-and yet they admit that he bound his father (Cronos) because he wickedly devoured his sons, and that he too had punished his own father (Uranus) for a similar reason, in a nameless manner. And yet when I proceed against my father, they are angry with me. So inconsistent are they in their way of talking when the gods are concerned, and when I am concerned.

Soc. May not this be the reason, Euthyphro, why I am charged with impiety-that I cannot away with these stories about the gods? and therefore I suppose that people think me wrong. But, as you who are well informed about them approve of them, I cannot do better than assent to your superior wisdom. What else can I say, confessing as I do, that I know nothing about them? Tell me, for the love of Zeus, whether you really believe that they are true.

Euth. Yes, Socrates; and things more wonderful still, of which the world is in ignorance.

Soc. And do you really believe that the gods, fought with one another, and had dire quarrels, battles, and the like, as the poets say, and as you may see represented in the works of great artists? The temples are full of them; and notably the robe of Athene, which is carried up to the Acropolis at the great Panathenaea, is embroidered with them. Are all these tales of the gods true, Euthyphro?

Euth. Yes, Socrates; and, as I was saying, I can tell you, if you would like to hear them, many other things about the gods which would quite amaze you.

Soc. I dare say; and you shall tell me them at some other time when I have leisure. But just at present I would rather hear from you a more precise answer, which you have not as yet given, my friend, to the question, What is "piety"? When asked, you only replied, Doing as you do, charging your father with murder.

Euth. And what I said was true, Socrates.

Soc. No doubt, Euthyphro; but you would admit that

there are many other pious acts?

Euth. There are.

Soc. Remember that I did not ask you to give me two or three examples of piety, but to explain the general idea which makes all pious things to be pious. Do you not recollect that there was one idea which made the impious impious, and the pious pious?

Euth. I remember.

Soc. Tell me what is the nature of this idea, and then I shall have a standard to which I may look, and by which I may measure actions, whether yours or those of any one else, and then I shall be able to say that such and such an action is pious, such another impious.

Euth. I will tell you, if you like.

Soc. I should very much like.

Euth. Piety, then, is that which is dear to the gods, and impiety is that which is not dear to them.

Soc. Very good, Euthyphro; you have now given me the sort of answer which I wanted. But whether what you say is true or not I cannot as yet tell, although I make no doubt that you will prove the truth of your words.

Euth. Of course.

Soc. Come, then, and let us examine what we are saying. That thing or person which is dear to the gods is pious, and that thing or person which is hateful to the gods is impious, these two being the extreme opposites of one another. Was not that said?

Euth. It was.

Soc. And well said?

Euth. Yes, Socrates, I thought so; it was certainly said.

Soc. And further, Euthyphro, the gods were admitted to

have enmities and hatreds and differences?

Euth. Yes, that was also said.

Soc. And what sort of difference creates enmity and anger? Suppose for example that you and I, my good friend, differ about a number; do differences of this sort make us enemies and set us at variance with one another? Do we not go at once to arithmetic, and put an end to them by a sum?

Euth. True.

Soc. Or suppose that we differ about magnitudes, do we not quickly end the differences by measuring?

Euth. Very true.

Soc. And we end a controversy about heavy and light by resorting to a weighing machine?

Euth. To be sure.

Soc. But what differences are there which cannot be thus decided, and which therefore make us angry and set us at enmity with one another? I dare say the answer does not occur to you at the moment, and therefore I will suggest that these enmities arise when the matters of difference are the just and unjust, good and evil, honourable and dishonourable. Are not these the points about which men differ, and about which when we are unable satisfactorily to decide our differences, you and I and all of us quarrel, when we do quarrel?

Euth. Yes, Socrates, the nature of the differences about which we quarrel is such as you describe.

Soc. And the quarrels of the gods, noble Euthyphro, when they occur, are of a like nature?

Euth. Certainly they are.

Soc. They have differences of opinion, as you say, about good and evil, just and unjust, honourable and dishonourable: there would have been no quarrels among them, if there had been no such differences-would there now?

Euth. You are quite right.

Soc. Does not every man love that which he deems noble and just and good, and hate the opposite of them?

Euth. Very true.

Soc. But, as you say, people regard the same things, some as just and others as unjust,-about these they dispute; and so there arise wars and fightings among them.

Euth. Very true.

Soc. Then the same things are hated by the gods and loved by the gods, and are both hateful and dear to them?

Euth. True.

Soc. And upon this view the same things, Euthyphro, will be pious and also impious?

Euth. So I should suppose.

Soc. Then, my friend, I remark with surprise that you have not answered the question which I asked. For I certainly did not ask you to tell me what action is both pious and impious: but now it would seem that what is loved by the gods is also hated by them. And therefore, Euthyphro, in thus chastising your father you may very likely be doing what is agreeable to Zeus but disagreeable to Cronos or Uranus, and what is acceptable to Hephaestus but unacceptable to Here, and there may be other gods who have similar differences of opinion.

Euth. But I believe, Socrates, that all the gods would be agreed as to the propriety of punishing a murderer: there would be no difference of opinion about that.

Soc. Well, but speaking of men, Euthyphro, did you ever hear any one arguing that a murderer or any sort of evil-doer ought to be let off?

Euth. I should rather say that these are the questions

which they are always arguing, especially in courts of law: they commit all sorts of crimes, and there is nothing which they will not do or say in their own defence.

Soc. But do they admit their guilt, Euthyphro, and yet say that they ought not to be punished?

Euth. No; they do not.

Soc. Then there are some things which they do not venture to say and do: for they do not venture to argue that the guilty are to be unpunished, but they deny their guilt, do they not?

Euth. Yes.

Soc. Then they do not argue that the evil-doer should not be punished, but they argue about the fact of who the evil-doer is, and what he did and when?

Euth. True.

Soc. And the gods are in the same case, if as you assert they quarrel about just and unjust, and some of them say while others deny that injustice is done among them. For surely neither God nor man will ever venture to say that the doer of injustice is not to be punished?

Euth. That is true, Socrates, in the main.

Soc. But they join issue about the particulars-gods and men alike; and, if they dispute at all, they dispute about some act which is called in question, and which by some is affirmed to be just, by others to be unjust. Is not that true?

Euth. Quite true.

Soc. Well then, my dear friend Euthyphro, do tell me, for my better instruction and information, what proof have you that in the opinion of all the gods a servant who is guilty of murder, and is put in chains by the master of the dead man, and dies because he is put in chains before he who bound him can learn from the interpreters of the gods what he ought to do with him, dies unjustly; and that on behalf of such an one a son ought to proceed against his father and accuse him of murder. How would you show that all the gods absolutely agree in approving of his act? Prove to me that they do, and I will applaud your wisdom as long as I live.

Euth. It will be a difficult task; but I could make the matter very dear indeed to you.

Soc. I understand; you mean to say that I am not so quick of apprehension as the judges: for to them you will be sure to prove that the act is unjust, and hateful to the gods.

Euth. Yes indeed, Socrates; at least if they will listen to me.

Soc. But they will be sure to listen if they find that you are a good speaker. There was a notion that came into my mind while you were speaking; I said to myself: "Well, and what if Euthyphro does prove to me that all the gods regarded the death of the serf as unjust, how do I know anything more of the nature of piety and impiety? for granting that this action may be hateful to the gods, still piety and impiety are not adequately defined by these distinctions, for that which is hateful to the gods has been shown to be also pleasing and dear to them." And therefore, Euthyphro, I do not ask you to prove this; I will suppose, if you like, that all the gods condemn and abominate such an action. But I will amend the definition so far as to say that what all the gods hate is impious, and what they love pious or holy; and what some of them love and others hate is both or neither. Shall this be our definition of piety and impiety?

Euth. Why not, Socrates?

Soc. Why not! certainly, as far as I am concerned, Euthyphro, there is no reason why not. But whether this admission will greatly assist you in the task of instructing me as you promised, is a matter for you to consider.

Euth. Yes, I should say that what all the gods love is pious and holy, and the opposite which they all hate, impious.

Soc. Ought we to enquire into the truth of this, Euthyphro, or simply to accept the mere statement on our own authority and that of others? What do you say?

Euth. We should enquire; and I believe that the statement will stand the test of enquiry.

Soc. We shall know better, my good friend, in a little while. The point which I should first wish to understand is whether the pious or holy is beloved by the gods because it is holy, or holy because it is beloved of the gods.

Euth. I do not understand your meaning, Socrates.

Soc. I will endeavour to explain: we, speak of carrying and we speak of being carried, of leading and being led, seeing and being seen. You know that in all such cases there is a difference, and you know also in what the difference lies?

Euth. I think that I understand.

Soc. And is not that which is beloved distinct from that which loves?

Euth. Certainly.

Soc. Well; and now tell me, is that which is carried in this state of carrying because it is carried, or for some other reason?

Euth. No; that is the reason.

Soc. And the same is true of what is led and of what is seen?

Euth. True.

Soc. And a thing is not seen because it is visible, but conversely, visible because it is seen; nor is a thing led because it is in the state of being led, or carried because it is in the state of being carried, but the converse of this. And now I think, Euthyphro, that my meaning will be intelligible; and my meaning is, that any state of action or passion implies previous action or passion. It does not become because it is becoming, but it is in a state of becoming because it becomes;

neither does it suffer because it is in a state of suffering, but it is in a state of suffering because it suffers. Do you not agree?

Euth. Yes.

Soc. Is not that which is loved in some state either of becoming or suffering?

Euth. Yes.

Soc. And the same holds as in the previous instances; the state of being loved follows the act of being loved, and not the act the state.

Euth. Certainly.

Soc. And what do you say of piety, Euthyphro: is not piety, according to your definition, loved by all the gods?

Euth. Yes.

Soc. Because it is pious or holy, or for some other reason?

Euth. No, that is the reason.

Soc. It is loved because it is holy, not holy because it is loved?

Euth. Yes.

Soc. And that which is dear to the gods is loved by them, and is in a state to be loved of them because it is loved of them?

Euth. Certainly.

Soc. Then that which is dear to the gods, Euthyphro, is not holy, nor is that which is holy loved of God, as you affirm; but they are two different things.

Euth. How do you mean, Socrates?

Soc. I mean to say that the holy has been acknowledge by us to be loved of God because it is holy, not to be holy because it is loved.

Euth. Yes.

Soc. But that which is dear to the gods is dear to them because it is loved by them, not loved by them because it is dear to them.

Euth. True.

Soc. But, friend Euthyphro, if that which is holy is the same with that which is dear to God, and is loved because it is holy, then that which is dear to God would have been loved as being dear to God; but if that which dear to God is dear to him because loved by him, then that which is holy would have been holy because loved by him. But now you see that the reverse is the case, and that they are quite different from one another. For one (theophiles) is of a kind to be loved cause it is loved, and the other (osion) is loved because it is of a kind to be loved. Thus you appear to me, Euthyphro, when I ask you what is the essence of holiness, to offer an attribute only, and not the essence-the attribute of being loved by all the gods. But you still refuse to explain to me the nature of holiness. And therefore, if you please, I will ask you not to hide your treasure, but to tell me once more what holiness or piety really is, whether dear to the gods or not (for that is a matter about which we will not quarrel) and what is impiety?

Euth. I really do not know, Socrates, how to express what I mean. For somehow or other our arguments, on whatever ground we rest them, seem to turn round and walk away from us.

Soc. Your words, Euthyphro, are like the handiwork of my ancestor Daedalus; and if I were the sayer or propounder of them, you might say that my arguments walk away and will not remain fixed where they are placed because I am a descendant of his. But now, since these notions are your own, you must find some other gibe, for they certainly, as you yourself allow, show an inclination to be on the move.

Euth. Nay, Socrates, I shall still say that you are the Daedalus who sets arguments in motion; not I, certainly, but you make them move or go round, for they would never have stirred, as far as I am concerned.

Soc. Then I must be a greater than Daedalus: for whereas he only made his own inventions to move, I move those of other people as well. And the beauty of it is, that I would rather not. For I would give the wisdom of Daedalus, and the wealth of Tantalus, to be able to detain them and keep them fixed. But enough of this. As I perceive that you are lazy, I will myself endeavor to show you how you might instruct me in the nature of piety; and I hope that you will not grudge your labour. Tell me, then-Is not that which is pious necessarily just?

Euth. Yes.

Soc. And is, then, all which is just pious? or, is that which is pious all just, but that which is just, only in part and not all, pious?

Euth. I do not understand you, Socrates.

Soc. And yet I know that you are as much wiser than I am, as you are younger. But, as I was saying, revered friend, the abundance of your wisdom makes you lazy. Please to exert yourself, for there is no real difficulty in understanding me. What I mean I may explain by an illustration of what I do not mean. The poet (Stasinus) sings-

Of Zeus, the author and creator of all these things,

You will not tell: for where there is fear there is also

reverence.

Now I disagree with this poet. Shall I tell you in what respect?

Euth. By all means.

Soc. I should not say that where there is fear there is also reverence; for I am sure that many persons fear poverty and disease, and the like evils, but I do not perceive that they reverence the objects of their fear.

Euth. Very true.

Soc. But where reverence is, there is fear; for he who has a feeling of reverence and shame about the commission of any action, fears and is afraid of an ill reputation.

Euth. No doubt.

Soc. Then we are wrong in saying that where there is fear there is also reverence; and we should say, where there is reverence there is also fear. But there is not always reverence where there is fear; for fear is a more extended notion, and reverence is a part of fear, just as the odd is a part of number, and number is a more extended notion than the odd. I suppose that you follow me now?

Euth. Quite well.

Soc. That was the sort of question which I meant to raise when I asked whether the just is always the pious, or the pious always the just; and whether there may not be justice where there is not piety; for justice is the more extended notion of which piety is only a part. Do you dissent?

Euth. No, I think that you are quite right.

Soc. Then, if piety is a part of justice, I suppose that we should enquire what part? If you had pursued the enquiry in the previous cases; for instance, if you had asked me what is an even number, and what part of number the even is, I should have had no difficulty in replying, a number which represents a figure having two equal sides. Do you not agree?

Euth. Yes, I quite agree.

Soc. In like manner, I want you to tell me what part of justice is piety or holiness, that I may be able to tell Meletus not to do me injustice, or indict me for impiety, as I am now adequately instructed by you in the nature of piety or holiness, and their opposites.

Euth. Piety or holiness, Socrates, appears to me to be that part of justice which attends to the gods, as there is the other part of justice which attends to men.

Soc. That is good, Euthyphro; yet still there is a little point about which I should like to have further information, What is the meaning of "attention"? For attention can hardly be used in the same sense when applied to the gods as when applied to other things. For instance, horses are said to require attention, and not every person is able to attend to them, but only a person skilled in horsemanship. Is it not so?

Euth. Certainly.

Soc. I should suppose that the art of horsemanship is the art of attending to horses?

Euth. Yes.

Soc. Nor is every one qualified to attend to dogs, but only the huntsman?

Euth. True.

Soc. And I should also conceive that the art of the huntsman is the art of attending to dogs?

Euth. Yes.

Soc. As the art of the ox herd is the art of attending to oxen?

Euth. Very true.

Soc. In like manner holiness or piety is the art of attending to the gods?-that would be your meaning, Euthyphro?

Euth. Yes.

Soc. And is not attention always designed for the good or benefit of that to which the attention is given? As in the case of horses, you may observe that when attended to by the horseman's art they are benefited and improved, are they not?

Euth. True.

Soc. As the dogs are benefited by the huntsman's art, and the oxen by the art of the ox herd, and all other things are tended or attended for their good and not for their hurt?

Euth. Certainly, not for their hurt.

Soc. But for their good?

Euth. Of course.

Soc. And does piety or holiness, which has been defined to be the art of attending to the gods, benefit or improve them? Would you say that when you do a holy act you make any of the gods better?

Euth. No, no; that was certainly not what I meant.

Soc. And I, Euthyphro, never supposed that you did. I asked you the question about the nature of the attention, because I thought that you did not.

Euth. You do me justice, Socrates; that is not the sort of attention which I mean.

Soc. Good: but I must still ask what is this attention to the gods which is called piety?

Euth. It is such, Socrates, as servants show to their masters.

Soc. I understand-a sort of ministration to the gods.

Euth. Exactly.

Soc. Medicine is also a sort of ministration or service, having in view the attainment of some object-would you not say of health?

Euth. I should.

Soc. Again, there is an art which ministers to the shipbuilder with a view to the attainment of some result?

Euth. Yes, Socrates, with a view to the building of a ship.

Soc. As there is an art which ministers to the house-builder with a view to the building of a house?

Euth. Yes.

Soc. And now tell me, my good friend, about the art which ministers to the gods: what work does that help to accomplish? For you must surely know if, as you say, you are of all men living the one who is best instructed in religion.

Euth. And I speak the truth, Socrates.

Soc. Tell me then, oh tell me-what is that fair work which the gods do by the help of our ministrations?

Euth. Many and fair, Socrates, are the works which they do.

Soc. Why, my friend, and so are those of a general. But the chief of them is easily told. Would you not say that victory in war is the chief of them?

Euth. Certainly.

Soc. Many and fair, too, are the works of the husband-man, if I am not mistaken; but his chief work is the production of food from the earth?

Euth. Exactly.

Soc. And of the many and fair things done by the gods, which is the chief or principal one?

Euth. I have told you already, Socrates, that to learn all these things accurately will be very tiresome. Let me simply say that piety or holiness is learning, how to please the gods in word and deed, by prayers and sacrifices. Such piety, is the salvation of families and states, just as the impious, which is unpleasing to the gods, is their ruin and destruction.

Soc. I think that you could have answered in much fewer words the chief question which I asked, Euthyphro, if you had chosen. But I see plainly that you are not disposed to instruct me-dearly not: else why, when we reached the point, did you turn, aside? Had you only answered me I should have truly learned of you by this time the-nature of piety. Now, as the asker of a question is necessarily dependent on the answerer, whither he leads-I must follow; and can only ask again, what is the pious, and what is piety? Do you mean that they are a, sort of science of praying and sacrificing?

Euth. Yes, I do.

Soc. And sacrificing is giving to the gods, and prayer is asking of the gods?

Euth. Yes, Socrates.

Soc. Upon this view, then piety is a science of asking and giving?

Euth. You understand me capitally, Socrates.

Soc. Yes, my friend; the. reason is that I am a votary of your science, and give my mind to it, and therefore nothing which you say will be thrown away upon me. Please then to tell me, what is the nature of this service to the gods? Do you mean that we prefer requests and give gifts to them?

Euth. Yes, I do.

Soc. Is not the right way of asking to ask of them what we want?

Euth. Certainly.

Soc. And the right way of giving is to give to them in return what they want of us. There would be no, in an art which gives to any one that which he does not want.

Euth. Very true, Socrates.

Soc. Then piety, Euthyphro, is an art which gods and men have of doing business with one another?

Euth. That is an expression which you may use, if you like.

Soc. But I have no particular liking for anything but the truth. I wish, however, that you would tell me what benefit accrues to the gods from our gifts. There is no doubt about what they give to us; for there is no good thing which they do not give; but how we can give any good thing to them in return is far from being equally clear. If they give everything and we give nothing, that must be an affair of business in which we have very greatly the advantage of them.

Euth. And do you imagine, Socrates, that any benefit accrues to the gods from our gifts?

Soc. But if not, Euthyphro, what is the meaning of gifts which are conferred by us upon the gods?

Euth. What else, but tributes of honour; and, as I was just now saying, what pleases them?

Soc. Piety, then, is pleasing to the gods, but not beneficial or dear to them?

Euth. I should say that nothing could be dearer.

Soc. Then once more the assertion is repeated that piety is dear to the gods?

Euth. Certainly.

Soc. And when you say this, can you wonder at your words not standing firm, but walking away? Will you accuse me of being the Daedalus who makes them walk away, not perceiving that there is another and far greater artist than Daedalus who makes them go round in a circle, and he is yourself; for the argument, as you will perceive, comes round to the same point. Were we not saying that the holy or pious was not the same with that which is loved of the gods? Have you forgotten?

Euth. I quite remember.

Soc. And are you not saying that what is loved of the

gods is holy; and is not this the same as what is dear to them- do you see?

Euth. True.

Soc. Then either we were wrong in former assertion; or, if we were right then, we are wrong now.

Euth. One of the two must be true.

Soc. Then we must begin again and ask, What is piety? That is an enquiry which I shall never be weary of pursuing as far as in me lies; and I entreat you not to scorn me, but to apply your mind to the utmost, and tell me the truth. For, if any man knows, you are he; and therefore I must detain you, like Proteus, until you tell. If you had not certainly known the nature of piety and impiety, I am confident that you would never, on behalf of a serf, have charged your aged father with murder. You would not have run such a risk of doing wrong in the sight of the gods, and you would have had too much respect for the opinions of men. I am sure, therefore, that you know the nature of piety and impiety. Speak out then, my dear Euthyphro, and do not hide your knowledge.

Euth. Another time, Socrates; for I am in a hurry, and must go now.

Soc. Alas! my companion, and will you leave me in de- spair? I was hoping that you would instruct me in the nature of piety and impiety; and then I might have cleared myself of Meletus and his indictment. I would have told him that I had been enlightened by Euthyphro, and had given up rash in- novations and speculations, in which I indulged only through ignorance, and that now I am about to lead a better life.

-THE END-

II.

Apology

INTRODUCTION

In what relation the Apology of Plato stands to the real defence of Socrates, there are no means of determining. It certainly agrees in tone and character with the description of Xenophon, who says in the Memorabilia that Socrates might have been acquitted 'if in any moderate degree he would have conciliated the favour of the dicasts;' and who informs us in another passage, on the testimony of Hermogenes, the friend of Socrates, that he had no wish to live; and that the divine sign refused to allow him to prepare a defence, and also that Socrates himself declared this to be unnecessary, on the ground that all his life long he had been preparing against that hour. For the speech breathes throughout a spirit of defiance, (ut non supplex aut reus sed magister aut dominus videretur esse judicum' (Cic. de Orat.); and the loose and desultory style is an imitation of the 'accustomed manner' in which Socrates spoke in 'the agora and among the tables of the money-changers.' The allusion in the Crito may, perhaps, be adduced as a further evidence of the literal accuracy of some parts. But in the main it must be regarded as the ideal of Socrates, according to Plato's conception of him, appearing in the greatest and most public scene of his life, and in the height of his triumph, when he is weakest, and yet his mastery over mankind is greatest, and his habitual irony acquires a new meaning and a sort of tragic pathos in the face of death. The facts of his life are summed up, and the features of his character are brought out as if by accident in the course of the defence. The conversational manner, the seeming want of arrangement, the ironical simplicity, are found to result in a perfect work of art, which is the portrait of Socrates.

Yet some of the topics may have been actually used by Socrates; and the recollection of his very words may have rung in the ears of his disciple. The Apology of Plato may be compared generally with those speeches of Thucydides in which he has embodied his conception of the lofty character and policy of the great Pericles, and which at the same time furnish a commentary on the situation of affairs from the

This is not history

point of view of the historian. So in the Apology there is an ideal rather than a literal truth; much is said which was not said, and is only Plato's view of the situation. Plato was not, like Xenophon, a chronicler of facts; he does not appear in any of his writings to have aimed at literal accuracy. He is not therefore to be supplemented from the Memorabilia and Symposium of Xenophon, who belongs to an entirely different class of writers. The Apology of Plato is not the report of what Socrates said, but an elaborate composition, quite as much so in fact as one of the Dialogues. And we may perhaps even indulge in the fancy that the actual defence of Socrates was as much greater than the Platonic defence as the master was greater than the disciple. But in any case, some of the words used by him must have been remembered, and some of the facts recorded must have actually occurred. It is significant that Plato is said to have been present at the defence (Apol.), as he is also said to have been absent at the last scene in the Phaedo. Is it fanciful to suppose that he meant to give the stamp of authenticity to the one and not to the other?--especially when we consider that these two passages are the only ones in which Plato makes mention of himself. The circumstance that Plato was to be one of his sureties for the payment of the fine which he proposed has the appearance of truth. More suspicious is the statement that Socrates received the first impulse to his favourite calling of cross-examining the world from the Oracle of Delphi; for he must already have been famous before Chaerephon went to consult the Oracle (Riddell), and the story is of a kind which is very likely to have been invented. On the whole we arrive at the conclusion that the Apology is true to the character of Socrates, but we cannot show that any single sentence in it was actually spoken by him. It breathes the spirit of Socrates, but has been cast anew in the mould of Plato.

Plato only mentions himself in two of his dialogues

How do we know which phrases are true

There is not much in the other Dialogues which can be compared with the Apology. The same recollection of his master may have been present to the mind of Plato when depicting the sufferings of the Just in the Republic. The Crito may also be regarded as a sort of appendage to the Apology, in which Socrates, who has defied the judges, is nevertheless represented as scrupulously obedient to the laws. The idealization of the sufferer is carried still further in the Gorgias, in which the thesis is maintained, that 'to suffer is better than to do evil;' and the art of rhetoric is described as only useful for the purpose of self-accusation. The parallelisms which occur in the so-called Apology of Xenophon are not worth noticing, because the writing in which they are contained is manifestly spurious. The statements of the Memorabilia respecting the trial and death of Socrates agree generally with Plato; but they have lost the flavour of Socratic irony in the narrative of Xenophon.

[handwritten marginal note: This dialogue highlights the suffering of the Just]

[handwritten note: (not exactly accurate; untrustworthy)]

The Apology or Platonic defence of Socrates is divided into three parts: 1st. The defence properly so called; 2nd. The shorter address in mitigation of the penalty; 3rd. The last words of prophetic rebuke and exhortation.

The first part commences with an apology for his colloquial style; he is, as he has always been, the enemy of rhetoric, and knows of no rhetoric but truth; he will not falsify his character by making a speech. Then he proceeds to divide his accusers into two classes; first, there is the nameless accuser--public opinion. All the world from their earliest years had heard that he was a corrupter of youth, and had seen him caricatured in the Clouds of Aristophanes. Secondly, there are the professed accusers, who are but the mouth-piece of the others. The accusations of both might be summed up in a formula. The first say, 'Socrates is an evil-doer and a curious person, searching into things under the earth and above the heaven; and making the worse appear the better cause, and teaching all this to others.' The second, 'Socrates is an evil-doer and corrupter of the youth, who does not receive the gods whom the state receives, but introduces other new divinities.' These last words appear to have been the actual indictment (compare Xen. Mem.); and the previous formula, which is a summary of public opinion, assumes the same legal style.

The answer begins by clearing up a confusion. In the representations of the Comic poets, and in the opinion of the multitude, he had been identified with the teachers of physi-

cal science and with the Sophists. But this was an error.
For both of them he professes a respect in the open court,
which contrasts with his manner of speaking about them in
other places. (Compare for Anaxagoras, Phaedo, Laws; for
the Sophists, Meno, Republic, Tim., Theaet., Soph., etc.) But
at the same time he shows that he is not one of them. Of
natural philosophy he knows nothing; not that he despises
such pursuits, but the fact is that he is ignorant of them,
and never says a word about them. Nor is he paid for giving
instruction--that is another mistaken notion:--he has nothing to teach. But he commends Evenus for teaching virtue
at such a 'moderate' rate as five minae. Something of the
'accustomed irony,' which may perhaps be expected to sleep
in the ear of the multitude, is lurking here.

He then goes on to explain the reason why he is in such an
evil name. That had arisen out of a peculiar mission which
he had taken upon himself. The enthusiastic Chaerephon
(probably in anticipation of the answer which he received)
had gone to Delphi and asked the oracle if there was any
man wiser than Socrates; and the answer was, that there was
no man wiser. What could be the meaning of this--that he
who knew nothing, and knew that he knew nothing, should
be declared by the oracle to be the wisest of men? Reflecting upon the answer, he determined to refute it by finding 'a
wiser;' and first he went to the politicians, and then to the
poets, and then to the craftsmen, but always with the same
result--he found that they knew nothing, or hardly anything
more than himself; and that the little advantage which in
some cases they possessed was more than counter-balanced
by their conceit of knowledge. He knew nothing, and knew
that he knew nothing: they knew little or nothing, and imagined that they knew all things. Thus he had passed his life
as a sort of missionary in detecting the pretended wisdom of
mankind; and this occupation had quite absorbed him and
taken him away both from public and private affairs. Young
men of the richer sort had made a pastime of the same pursuit, 'which was not unamusing.' And hence bitter enmities
had arisen; the professors of knowledge had revenged themselves by calling him a villainous corrupter of youth, and by

repeating the commonplaces about atheism and materialism and sophistry, which are the stock-accusations against all philosophers when there is nothing else to be said of them.

The second accusation he meets by interrogating Meletus, who is present and can be interrogated. 'If he is the corrupter, who is the improver of the citizens?' (Compare Meno.) 'All men everywhere.' But how absurd, how contrary to analogy is this! How inconceivable too, that he should make the citizens worse when he has to live with them. This surely cannot be intentional; and if unintentional, he ought to have been instructed by Meletus, and not accused in the court.

But there is another part of the indictment which says that he teaches men not to receive the gods whom the city receives, and has other new gods. 'Is that the way in which he is supposed to corrupt the youth?' 'Yes, it is.' 'Has he only new gods, or none at all?' 'None at all.' 'What, not even the sun and moon?' 'No; why, he says that the sun is a stone, and the moon earth.' That, replies Socrates, is the old confusion about Anaxagoras; the Athenian people are not so ignorant as to attribute to the influence of Socrates notions which have found their way into the drama, and may be learned at the theatre. Socrates undertakes to show that Meletus (rather unjustifiably) has been compounding a riddle in this part of the indictment: 'There are no gods, but Socrates believes in the existence of the sons of gods, which is absurd.'

Leaving Meletus, who has had enough words spent upon him, he returns to the original accusation. The question may be asked, Why will he persist in following a profession which leads him to death? Why?--because he must remain at his post where the god has placed him, as he remained at Potidaea, and Amphipolis, and Delium, where the generals placed him. Besides, he is not so overwise as to imagine that he knows whether death is a good or an evil; and he is certain that desertion of his duty is an evil. Anytus is quite right in saying that they should never have indicted him if they meant to let him go. For he will certainly obey God rather than man; and will continue to preach to all men of all ages the necessity of virtue and improvement; and if they refuse to listen to him he will still persevere and reprove them. This is his way of corrupting the youth, which he will not cease to follow in obedience to the god, even if a thousand deaths await him.

He is desirous that they should let him live--not for his own sake, but for theirs; because he is their heaven-sent friend (and they will never have such another), or, as he may be ludicrously described, he is the gadfly who stirs the generous steed into motion. Why then has he never taken part in public affairs? Because the familiar divine voice has hindered him; if he had been a public man, and had fought for the right, as he would certainly have fought against the many, he would not have lived, and could therefore have done no good. Twice in public matters he has risked his life for the sake of justice--once at the trial of the generals; and again in resistance to the tyrannical commands of the Thirty.

But, though not a public man, he has passed his days in instructing the citizens without fee or reward--this was his mission. Whether his disciples have turned out well or ill, he cannot justly be charged with the result, for he never promised to teach them anything. They might come if they liked, and they might stay away if they liked: and they did come, because they found an amusement in hearing the pretenders to wisdom detected. If they have been corrupted, their elder relatives (if not themselves) might surely come into court and witness against him, and there is an opportunity still for them to appear. But their fathers and brothers all appear in court (including 'this' Plato), to witness on his behalf; and if their relatives are corrupted, at least they are uncorrupted; 'and they are my witnesses. For they know that I am speaking the truth, and that Meletus is lying.'

This is about all that he has to say. He will not entreat the judges to spare his life; neither will he present a spectacle of weeping children, although he, too, is not made of 'rock or oak.' Some of the judges themselves may have complied with this practice on similar occasions, and he trusts that they will not be angry with him for not following their example. But he feels that such conduct brings discredit on the name of Athens: he feels too, that the judge has sworn not to give away justice; and he cannot be guilty of the impiety of asking the judge to break his oath, when he is himself being tried for impiety.

As he expected, and probably intended, he is convicted. And now the tone of the speech, instead of being more conciliatory, becomes more lofty and commanding. Anytus proposes death as the penalty: and what counter- proposition shall he make? He, the benefactor of the Athenian people, whose whole life has been spent in doing them good, should at least have the Olympic victor's reward of maintenance in the Prytaneum. Or why should he propose any counter-penalty when he does not know whether death, which Anytus proposes, is a good or an evil? And he is certain that imprisonment is an evil, exile is an evil. Loss of money might be an evil, but then he has none to give; perhaps he can make up a mina. Let that be the penalty, or, if his friends wish, thirty minae; for which they will be excellent securities.

(He is condemned to death.)

He is an old man already, and the Athenians will gain nothing but disgrace by depriving him of a few years of life. Perhaps he could have escaped, if he had chosen to throw down his arms and entreat for his life. But he does not at all repent of the manner of his defence; he would rather die in his own fashion than live in theirs. For the penalty of unrighteousness is swifter than death; that penalty has already overtaken his accusers as death will soon overtake him.

And now, as one who is about to die, he will prophesy to them. They have put him to death in order to escape the necessity of giving an account of their lives. But his death 'will be the seed' of many disciples who will convince them of their evil ways, and will come forth to reprove them in harsher terms, because they are younger and more inconsiderate.

He would like to say a few words, while there is time, to those who would have acquitted him. He wishes them

to know that the divine sign never interrupted him in the
course of his defence; the reason of which, as he conjectures,
is that the death to which he is going is a good and not an
evil. For either death is a long sleep, the best of sleeps, or a
journey to another world in which the souls of the dead are
gathered together, and in which there may be a hope of seeing the heroes of old--in which, too, there are just judges; and
as all are immortal, there can be no fear of any one suffering
death for his opinions.

Nothing evil can happen to the good man either in life or
death, and his own death has been permitted by the gods,
because it was better for him to depart; and therefore he for-
gives his judges because they have done him no harm, although they never meant to do him any good.

He has a last request to make to them--that they will
trouble his sons as he has troubled them, if they appear to
prefer riches to virtue, or to think themselves something
when they are nothing.

...

'Few persons will be found to wish that Socrates should
have defended himself otherwise,'--if, as we must add, his defence was that with which Plato has provided him. But leaving this question, which does not admit of a precise solution,
we may go on to ask what was the impression which Plato
in the Apology intended to give of the character and conduct
of his master in the last great scene? Did he intend to represent him (1) as employing sophistries; (2) as designedly irritating the judges? Or are these sophistries to be regarded
as belonging to the age in which he lived and to his personal
character, and this apparent haughtiness as flowing from
the natural elevation of his position?

For example, when he says that it is absurd to suppose
that one man is the corrupter and all the rest of the world
the improvers of the youth; or, when he argues that he never
could have corrupted the men with whom he had to live; or,
when he proves his belief in the gods because he believes in

the sons of gods, is he serious or jesting? It may be observed
that these sophisms all occur in his cross-examination of Meletus, who is easily foiled and mastered in the hands of the
great dialectician. Perhaps he regarded these answers as
good enough for his accuser, of whom he makes very light.
Also there is a touch of irony in them, which takes them out
of the category of sophistry. (Compare Euthyph.)

That the manner in which he defends himself about the
lives of his disciples is not satisfactory, can hardly be denied.
Fresh in the memory of the Athenians, and detestable as
they deserved to be to the newly restored democracy, were
the names of Alcibiades, Critias, Charmides. It is obviously
not a sufficient answer that Socrates had never professed
to teach them anything, and is therefore not justly charge-
able with their crimes. Yet the defence, when taken out of
this ironical form, is doubtless sound: that his teaching had
nothing to do with their evil lives. Here, then, the sophistry
is rather in form than in substance, though we might desire
that to such a serious charge Socrates had given a more serious answer.

Truly characteristic of Socrates is another point in his
answer, which may also be regarded as sophistical. He says
that 'if he has corrupted the youth, he must have corrupted
them involuntarily.' But if, as Socrates argues, all evil is
involuntary, then all criminals ought to be admonished and
not punished. In these words the Socratic doctrine of the
involuntariness of evil is clearly intended to be conveyed.
Here again, as in the former instance, the defence of Socrates is untrue practically, but may be true in some ideal
or transcendental sense. The commonplace reply, that if he
had been guilty of corrupting the youth their relations would
surely have witnessed against him, with which he concludes
this part of his defence, is more satisfactory.

Again, when Socrates argues that he must believe in the
gods because he believes in the sons of gods, we must remember that this is a refutation not of the original indictment,
which is consistent enough--'Socrates does not receive the
gods whom the city receives, and has other new divinities'

--but of the interpretation put upon the words by Meletus, who has affirmed that he is a downright atheist. To this Socrates fairly answers, in accordance with the ideas of the time, that a downright atheist cannot believe in the sons of gods or in divine things. The notion that demons or lesser divinities are the sons of gods is not to be regarded as ironical or sceptical. He is arguing 'ad hominem' according to the notions of mythology current in his age. Yet he abstains from saying that he believed in the gods whom the State approved. He does not defend himself, as Xenophon has defended him, by appealing to his practice of religion. Probably he neither wholly believed, nor disbelieved, in the existence of the popular gods; he had no means of knowing about them. According to Plato (compare Phaedo; Symp.), as well as Xenophon (Memor.), he was punctual in the performance of the least religious duties; and he must have believed in his own oracular sign, of which he seemed to have an internal witness. But the existence of Apollo or Zeus, or the other gods whom the State approves, would have appeared to him both uncertain and unimportant in comparison of the duty of self-examination, and of those principles of truth and right which he deemed to be the foundation of religion. (Compare Phaedr.; Euthyph.; Republic.)

The second question, whether Plato meant to represent Socrates as braving or irritating his judges, must also be answered in the negative. His irony, his superiority, his audacity, 'regarding not the person of man,' necessarily flow out of the loftiness of his situation.

He is not acting a part upon a great occasion, but he is what he has been all his life long, 'a king of men.' He would rather not appear insolent, if he could avoid it (ouch os authadizomenos touto lego). Neither is he desirous of hastening his own end, for life and death are simply indifferent to him.

But such a defence as would be acceptable to his judges and might procure an acquittal, it is not in his nature to make. He will not say or do anything that might pervert the course of justice; he cannot have his tongue bound even 'in the throat of death.'

With his accusers he will only fence and play, as he had fenced with other 'improvers of youth,' answering the Sophist according to his sophistry all his life long. He is serious when he is speaking of his own mission, which seems to distinguish him from all other reformers of mankind, and originates in an accident.

The dedication of himself to the improvement of his fellow-citizens is not so remarkable as the ironical spirit in which he goes about doing good only in vindication of the credit of the oracle, and in the vain hope of finding a wiser man than himself. Yet this singular and almost accidental character of his mission agrees with the divine sign which, according to our notions, is equally accidental and irrational, and is nevertheless accepted by him as the guiding principle of his life. Socrates is nowhere represented to us as a freethinker or sceptic. There is no reason to doubt his sincerity when he speculates on the possibility of seeing and knowing the heroes of the Trojan war in another world. On the other hand, his hope of immortality is uncertain;--he also conceives of death as a long sleep (in this respect differing from the Phaedo), and at last falls back on resignation to the divine will, and the certainty that no evil can happen to the good man either in life or death. His absolute truthfulness seems to hinder him from asserting positively more than this; and he makes no attempt to veil his ignorance in mythology and figures of speech. The gentleness of the first part of the speech contrasts with the aggravated, almost threatening, tone of the conclusion.

He characteristically remarks that he will not speak as a rhetorician, that is to say, he will not make a regular defence such as Lysias or one of the orators might have composed for him, or, according to some accounts, did compose for him. But he first procures himself a hearing by conciliatory words. He does not attack the Sophists; for they were open to the same charges as himself; they were equally ridiculed by the Comic poets, and almost equally hateful to Anytus and Meletus. Yet incidentally the antagonism between Socrates and the Sophists is allowed to appear. He is poor and they are rich; his profession that he teaches nothing is opposed to their readiness to teach all things; his talking in the marketplace to their private instructions; his tarry-at-home life to their wandering from city to city. The tone which he assumes towards them is one of real friendliness, but also of concealed irony. Towards Anaxagoras, who had disappointed him in his hopes of learning about mind and nature, he shows a less kindly feeling, which is also the feeling of Plato in other passages (Laws). But Anaxagoras had been dead thirty years, and was beyond the reach of persecution.

It has been remarked that the prophecy of a new generation of teachers who would rebuke and exhort the Athenian people in harsher and more violent terms was, as far as we know, never fulfilled. No inference can be drawn from this circumstance as to the probability of the words attributed to him having been actually uttered. They express the aspiration of the first martyr of philosophy, that he would leave behind him many followers, accompanied by the not unnatural feeling that they would be fiercer and more inconsiderate in their words when emancipated from his control.

The above remarks must be understood as applying with any degree of certainty to the Platonic Socrates only. For, although these or similar words may have been spoken by Socrates himself, we cannot exclude the possibility, that like so much else, e.g. the wisdom of Critias, the poem of Solon, the virtues of Charmides, they may have been due only to the imagination of Plato. The arguments of those who maintain that the Apology was composed during the process, resting on no evidence, do not require a serious refutation. Nor are the reasonings of Schleiermacher, who argues that the Platonic defence is an exact or nearly exact reproduction of the words of Socrates, partly because Plato would not have been guilty of the impiety of altering them, and also because many points of the defence might have been improved and strengthened, at all more conclusive. (See English Translation.) What effect the death of Socrates produced on the mind of Plato, we cannot certainly determine; nor can we say how he would or must have written under the circumstances. We observe that the enmity of Aristophanes to Socrates does not prevent Plato from introducing them together in the Symposium engaged in friendly intercourse. Nor is there any trace in the Dialogues of an attempt to make Anytus or Meletus personally odious in the eyes of the Athenian public.

APOLOGY

by

Plato

(Socrates is talking)

How you, O Athenians, have been affected by my accusers, I cannot tell; but I know that they almost made me forget who I was--so persuasively did they speak; and yet they have hardly uttered a word of truth. But of the many falsehoods told by them, there was one which quite amazed me;--I mean when they said that you should be upon your guard and not allow yourselves to be deceived by the force of my eloquence. To say this, when they were certain to be detected as soon as I opened my lips and proved myself to be anything but a great speaker, did indeed appear to me most shameless-- unless by the force of eloquence they mean the force of truth; for is such is their meaning, I admit that I am eloquent. But in how different a way from theirs! Well, as I was saying, they have scarcely spoken the truth at all; but from me you shall hear the whole truth: not, however, delivered after their manner in a set oration duly ornamented with words and phrases. No, by heaven! but I shall use the words and arguments which occur to me at the moment; for I am confident in the justice of my cause (Or, I am certain that I am right in taking this course.): at my time of life I ought not to be appearing before you, O men of Athens, in the character of a juvenile orator--let no one expect it of me. And I must beg of you to grant me a favour:--If I defend myself in my accustomed manner, and you hear me using the words which I have been in the habit of using in the agora, at the tables of the money-changers, or anywhere else, I would ask you not to be surprised, and not to interrupt me on this account. For I am more than seventy years of age, and appearing now for the first time in a court of law, I am quite a stranger to the language of the place; and therefore I would have you regard me as if I were really a stranger, whom you would ex-

does anyone else fear a little attitude

cuse if he spoke in his native tongue, and after the fashion of his country:--Am I making an unfair request of you? Never mind the manner, which may or may not be good; but think only of the truth of my words, and give heed to that: let the speaker speak truly and the judge decide justly.

And first, I have to reply to the older charges and to my first accusers, and then I will go on to the later ones. For of old I have had many accusers, who have accused me false-ly to you during many years; and I am more afraid of them than of Anytus and his associates, who are dangerous, too, in their own way. But far more dangerous are the others, who began when you were children, and took possession of your minds with their falsehoods, telling of one Socrates, a wise man, who speculated about the heaven above, and searched into the earth beneath, and made the worse appear the bet-ter cause. The disseminators of this tale are the accusers whom I dread; for their hearers are apt to fancy that such enquirers do not believe in the existence of the gods. And they are many, and their charges against me are of ancient date, and they were made by them in the days when you were more impressible than you are now--in childhood, or it may have been in youth--and the cause when heard went by default, for there was none to answer. And hardest of all, I do not know and cannot tell the names of my accusers; unless in the chance case of a Comic poet. All who from envy and malice have persuaded you--some of them having first con-vinced themselves--all this class of men are most difficult to deal with; for I cannot have them up here, and cross-examine them, and therefore I must simply fight with shadows in my own defence, and argue when there is no one who answers. I will ask you then to assume with me, as I was saying, that my opponents are of two kinds; one recent, the other ancient: and I hope that you will see the propriety of my answering the latter first, for these accusations you heard long before the others, and much oftener.

Well, then, I must make my defence, and endeavour to clear away in a short time, a slander which has lasted a long time. May I succeed, if to succeed be for my good and yours, or likely to avail me in my cause! The task is not an easy one; I quite understand the nature of it. And so leaving the event with God, in obedience to the law I will now make my defence.

I will begin at the beginning, and ask what is the accusation which has given rise to the slander of me, and in fact has encouraged Meletus to proof this charge against me. Well, what do the slanderers say? They shall be my prosecutors, and I will sum up their words in an affidavit: 'Socrates is an evil-doer, and a curious person, who searches into things under the earth and in heaven, and he makes the worse appear the better cause; and he teaches the aforesaid doctrines to others.' Such is the nature of the accusation: it is just what you have yourselves seen in the comedy of Aristophanes (Aristoph., Clouds.), who has introduced a man whom he calls Socrates, going about and saying that he walks in air, and talking a deal of nonsense concerning matters of which I do not pretend to know either much or little--not that I mean to speak disparagingly of any one who is a student of natural philosophy. I should be very sorry if Meletus could bring so grave a charge against me. But the simple truth is, O Athenians, that I have nothing to do with physical speculations. Very many of those here present are witnesses to the truth of this, and to them I appeal. Speak then, you who have heard me, and tell your neighbours whether any of you have ever known me hold forth in few words or in many upon such matters...You hear their answer. And from what they say of this part of the charge you will be able to judge of the truth of the rest.

As little foundation is there for the report that I am a teacher, and take money; this accusation has no more truth in it than the other. Although, if a man were really able to instruct mankind, to receive money for giving instruction would, in my opinion, be an honour to him. There is Gorgias of Leontium, and Prodicus of Ceos, and Hippias of Elis, who go the round of the cities, and are able to persuade the young men to leave their own citizens by whom they might be taught for nothing, and come to them whom they not only pay, but

are thankful if they may be allowed to pay them. There is at
this time a Parian philosopher residing in Athens, of whom
I have heard; and I came to hear of him in this way:--I came
across a man who has spent a world of money on the Sophists, Callias, the son of Hipponicus, and knowing that he had
sons, I asked him: 'Callias,' I said, 'if your two sons were foals
or calves, there would be no difficulty in finding some one to
put over them; we should hire a trainer of horses, or a farmer
probably, who would improve and perfect them in their own
proper virtue and excellence; but as they are human beings,
whom are you thinking of placing over them? Is there any
one who understands human and political virtue? You must
have thought about the matter, for you have sons; is there
any one?' 'There is,' he said. 'Who is he?' said I; 'and of what
country? and what does he charge?' 'Evenus the Parian,' he
replied; 'he is the man, and his charge is five minae.' Happy
is Evenus, I said to myself, if he really has this wisdom, and
teaches at such a moderate charge. Had I the same, I should
have been very proud and conceited; but the truth is that I
have no knowledge of the kind.

I dare say, Athenians, that some one among you will reply, 'Yes, Socrates, but what is the origin of these accusations
which are brought against you; there must have been something strange which you have been doing? All these rumours
and this talk about you would never have arisen if you had
been like other men: tell us, then, what is the cause of them,
for we should be sorry to judge hastily of you.' Now I regard
this as a fair challenge, and I will endeavour to explain to
you the reason why I am called wise and have such an evil
fame. Please to attend then. And although some of you may
think that I am joking, I declare that I will tell you the entire
truth. Men of Athens, this reputation of mine has come of a
certain sort of wisdom which I possess. If you ask me what
kind of wisdom, I reply, wisdom such as may perhaps be attained by man, for to that extent I am inclined to believe that
I am wise; whereas the persons of whom I was speaking have
a superhuman wisdom which I may fail to describe, because
I have it not myself; and he who says that I have, speaks
falsely, and is taking away my character. And here, O men

of Athens, I must beg you not to interrupt me, even if I seem
to say something extravagant. For the word which I will
speak is not mine. I will refer you to a witness who is worthy
of credit; that witness shall be the God of Delphi--he will tell
you about my wisdom, if I have any, and of what sort it is.
You must have known Chaerephon; he was early a friend of
mine, and also a friend of yours, for he shared in the recent
exile of the people, and returned with you. Well, Chaerephon, as you know, was very impetuous in all his doings,
and he went to Delphi and boldly asked the oracle to tell him
whether--as I was saying, I must beg you not to interrupt--he
asked the oracle to tell him whether anyone was wiser than
I was, and the Pythian prophetess answered, that there was
no man wiser. Chaerephon is dead himself; but his brother,
who is in court, will confirm the truth of what I am saying.

Why do I mention this? Because I am going to explain
to you why I have such an evil name. When I heard the
answer, I said to myself, What can the god mean? and what
is the interpretation of his riddle? for I know that I have no
wisdom, small or great. What then can he mean when he
says that I am the wisest of men? And yet he is a god, and
cannot lie; that would be against his nature. After long consideration, I thought of a method of trying the question. I reflected that if I could only find a man wiser than myself, then
I might go to the god with a refutation in my hand. I should
say to him, 'Here is a man who is wiser than I am; but you
said that I was the wisest.' Accordingly I went to one who
had the reputation of wisdom, and observed him--his name
I need not mention; he was a politician whom I selected for
examination--and the result was as follows: When I began
to talk with him, I could not help thinking that he was not
really wise, although he was thought wise by many, and still
wiser by himself; and thereupon I tried to explain to him
that he thought himself wise, but was not really wise; and
the consequence was that he hated me, and his enmity was
shared by several who were present and heard me. So I left
him, saying to myself, as I went away: Well, although I do
not suppose that either of us knows anything really beautiful
and good, I am better off than he is,-- for he knows nothing,

and thinks that he knows; I neither know nor think that I know. In this latter particular, then, I seem to have slightly the advantage of him. Then I went to another who had still higher pretensions to wisdom, and my conclusion was exactly the same. Whereupon I made another enemy of him, and of many others besides him.

Then I went to one man after another, being not unconscious of the enmity which I provoked, and I lamented and feared this: but necessity was laid upon me,--the word of God, I thought, ought to be considered first. And I said to myself, Go I must to all who appear to know, and find out the meaning of the oracle. And I swear to you, Athenians, by the dog I swear! --for I must tell you the truth--the result of my mission was just this: I found that the men most in repute were all but the most foolish; and that others less esteemed were really wiser and better. I will tell you the tale of my wanderings and of the 'Herculean' labours, as I may call them, which I endured only to find at last the oracle irrefutable. After the politicians, I went to the poets; tragic, dithyrambic, and all sorts. And there, I said to myself, you will be instantly detected; now you will find out that you are more ignorant than they are. Accordingly, I took them some of the most elaborate passages in their own writings, and asked what was the meaning of them--thinking that they would teach me something. Will you believe me? I am almost ashamed to confess the truth, but I must say that there is hardly a person present who would not have talked better about their poetry than they did themselves. Then I knew that not by wisdom do poets write poetry, but by a sort of genius and inspiration; they are like diviners or soothsayers who also say many fine things, but do not understand the meaning of them. The poets appeared to me to be much in the same case; and I further observed that upon the strength of their poetry they believed themselves to be the wisest of men in other things in which they were not wise. So I departed, conceiving myself to be superior to them for the same reason that I was superior to the politicians.

At last I went to the artisans. I was conscious that I

knew nothing at all, as I may say, and I was sure that they knew many fine things; and here I was not mistaken, for they did know many things of which I was ignorant, and in this they certainly were wiser than I was. But I observed that even the good artisans fell into the same error as the poets;--because they were good workmen they thought that they also knew all sorts of high matters, and this defect in them overshadowed their wisdom; and therefore I asked myself on behalf of the oracle, whether I would like to be as I was, neither having their knowledge nor their ignorance, or like them in both; and I made answer to myself and to the oracle that I was better off as I was.

[margin note: Because they really understood their craft, they think they know more than they do outside of their craft]

This inquisition has led to my having many enemies of the worst and most dangerous kind, and has given occasion also to many calumnies. And I am called wise, for my hearers always imagine that I myself possess the wisdom which I find wanting in others: but the truth is, O men of Athens, that God only is wise; and by his answer he intends to show that the wisdom of men is worth little or nothing; he is not speaking of Socrates, he is only using my name by way of illustration, as if he said, He, O men, is the wisest, who, like Socrates, knows that his wisdom is in truth worth nothing. And so I go about the world, obedient to the god, and search and make enquiry into the wisdom of any one, whether citizen or stranger, who appears to be wise; and if he is not wise, then in vindication of the oracle I show him that he is not wise; and my occupation quite absorbs me, and I have no time to give either to any public matter of interest or to any concern of my own, but I am in utter poverty by reason of my devotion to the god.

There is another thing:--young men of the richer classes, who have not much to do, come about me of their own accord; they like to hear the pretenders examined, and they often imitate me, and proceed to examine others; there are plenty of persons, as they quickly discover, who think that they know something, but really know little or nothing; and then those who are examined by them instead of being angry with themselves are angry with me: This confounded

Socrates, they say; this villainous misleader of youth!-- and
then if somebody asks them, Why, what evil does he prac-
tise or teach? they do not know, and cannot tell; but in order
that they may not appear to be at a loss, they repeat the
ready-made charges which are used against all philosophers
about teaching things up in the clouds and under the earth,
and having no gods, and making the worse appear the better cause; for they do not like to confess that their pretence
of knowledge has been detected-- which is the truth; and as
they are numerous and ambitious and energetic, and are
drawn up in battle array and have persuasive tongues, they
have filled your ears with their loud and inveterate calumnies. And this is the reason why my three accusers, Meletus
and Anytus and Lycon, have set upon me; Meletus, who has
a quarrel with me on behalf of the poets; Anytus, on behalf of
the craftsmen and politicians; Lycon, on behalf of the rheto-
ricians: and as I said at the beginning, I cannot expect to get
rid of such a mass of calumny all in a moment. And this, O
men of Athens, is the truth and the whole truth; I have concealed nothing, I have dissembled nothing. And yet, I know
that my plainness of speech makes them hate me, and what
is their hatred but a proof that I am speaking the truth?--
Hence has arisen the prejudice against me; and this is the
reason of it, as you will find out either in this or in any future
enquiry.

I have said enough in my defence against the first class
of my accusers; I turn to the second class. They are headed
by Meletus, that good man and true lover of his country, as
he calls himself. Against these, too, I must try to make a
defence:--Let their affidavit be read: it contains something of
this kind: It says that Socrates is a doer of evil, who corrupts
the youth; and who does not believe in the gods of the state,
but has other new divinities of his own. Such is the charge;
and now let us examine the particular counts. He says that I
am a doer of evil, and corrupt the youth; but I say, O men of
Athens, that Meletus is a doer of evil, in that he pretends to
be in earnest when he is only in jest, and is so eager to bring
men to trial from a pretended zeal and interest about matters in which he really never had the smallest interest. And

[handwritten margin note: Socrates had made many enemies out of the people he questioned]

the truth of this I will endeavour to prove to you.

Come hither, Meletus, and let me ask a question of you. You think a great deal about the improvement of youth?

Yes, I do.

Tell the judges, then, who is their improver; for you must know, as you have taken the pains to discover their corrupter, and are citing and accusing me before them. Speak, then, and tell the judges who their improver is.--Observe, Meletus, that you are silent, and have nothing to say. But is not this rather disgraceful, and a very considerable proof of what I was saying, that you have no interest in the matter? Speak up, friend, and tell us who their improver is.

The laws.

But that, my good sir, is not my meaning. I want to know who the person is, who, in the first place, knows the laws.

The judges, Socrates, who are present in court.

What, do you mean to say, Meletus, that they are able to instruct and improve youth?

Certainly they are.

What, all of them, or some only and not others?

All of them.

By the goddess Here, that is good news! There are plenty of improvers, then. And what do you say of the audience,--do they improve them?

Yes, they do.

And the senators?

Yes, the senators improve them.

But perhaps the members of the assembly corrupt them?--or do they too improve them?

They improve them.

Then every Athenian improves and elevates them; all with the exception of myself; and I alone am their corrupter? Is that what you affirm?

That is what I stoutly affirm.

I am very unfortunate if you are right. But suppose I ask you a question: How about horses? Does one man do them harm and all the world good? Is not the exact opposite the truth? One man is able to do them good, or at least not many;--the trainer of horses, that is to say, does them good, and others who have to do with them rather injure them? Is not that true, Meletus, of horses, or of any other animals? Most assuredly it is; whether you and Anytus say yes or no. Happy indeed would be the condition of youth if they had one corrupter only, and all the rest of the world were their improvers. But you, Meletus, have sufficiently shown that you never had a thought about the young: your carelessness is seen in your not caring about the very things which you bring against me.

And now, Meletus, I will ask you another question--by Zeus I will: Which is better, to live among bad citizens, or among good ones? Answer, friend, I say; the question is one which may be easily answered. Do not the good do their neighbours good, and the bad do them evil?

Certainly.

And is there anyone who would rather be injured than benefited by those who live with him? Answer, my good friend, the law requires you to answer-- does any one like to be injured?

Certainly not.

And when you accuse me of corrupting and deteriorating the youth, do you allege that I corrupt them intentionally or unintentionally?

Intentionally, I say.

But you have just admitted that the good do their neigh-

bours good, and the evil do them evil. Now, is that a truth
which your superior wisdom has recognized thus early in
life, and am I, at my age, in such darkness and ignorance
as not to know that if a man with whom I have to live is corrupted by me, I am very likely to be harmed by him; and yet
I corrupt him, and intentionally, too--so you say, although
neither I nor any other human being is ever likely to be convinced by you. But either I do not corrupt them, or I corrupt them unintentionally; and on either view of the case
you lie. If my offence is unintentional, the law has no cog-
nizance of unintentional offences: you ought to have taken
me privately, and warned and admonished me; for if I had
been better advised, I should have left off doing what I only
did unintentionally--no doubt I should; but you would have
nothing to say to me and refused to teach me. And now you
bring me up in this court, which is a place not of instruction,
but of punishment.

It will be very clear to you, Athenians, as I was saying,
that Meletus has no care at all, great or small, about the
matter. But still I should like to know, Meletus, in what I am
affirmed to corrupt the young. I suppose you mean, as I infer
from your indictment, that I teach them not to acknowledge
the gods which the state acknowledges, but some other new
divinities or spiritual agencies in their stead. These are the
lessons by which I corrupt the youth, as you say.

Yes, that I say emphatically.

Then, by the gods, Meletus, of whom we are speaking,
tell me and the court, in somewhat plainer terms, what you
mean! for I do not as yet understand whether you affirm that
I teach other men to acknowledge some gods, and therefore
that I do believe in gods, and am not an entire atheist--this
you do not lay to my charge,--but only you say that they are
not the same gods which the city recognizes--the charge is
that they are different gods. Or, do you mean that I am an
atheist simply, and a teacher of atheism?

I mean the latter--that you are a complete atheist.

What an extraordinary statement! Why do you think so, Meletus? Do you mean that I do not believe in the godhead of the sun or moon, like other men?

I assure you, judges, that he does not: for he says that the sun is stone, and the moon earth.

Friend Meletus, you think that you are accusing Anaxagoras: and you have but a bad opinion of the judges, if you fancy them illiterate to such a degree as not to know that these doctrines are found in the books of Anaxagoras the Clazomenian, which are full of them. And so, forsooth, the youth are said to be taught them by Socrates, when there are not unfrequently exhibitions of them at the theatre (Probably in allusion to Aristophanes who caricatured, and to Euripides who borrowed the notions of Anaxagoras, as well as to other dramatic poets.) (price of admission one drachma at the most); and they might pay their money, and laugh at Socrates if he pretends to father these extraordinary views. And so, Meletus, you really think that I do not believe in any god?

I swear by Zeus that you believe absolutely in none at all.

Nobody will believe you, Meletus, and I am pretty sure that you do not believe yourself. I cannot help thinking, men of Athens, that Meletus is reckless and impudent, and that he has written this indictment in a spirit of mere wantonness and youthful bravado. Has he not compounded a riddle, thinking to try me? He said to himself:--I shall see whether the wise Socrates will discover my facetious contradiction, or whether I shall be able to deceive him and the rest of them. For he certainly does appear to me to contradict himself in the indictment as much as if he said that Socrates is guilty of not believing in the gods, and yet of believing in them--but this is not like a person who is in earnest.

I should like you, O men of Athens, to join me in examining what I conceive to be his inconsistency; and do you, Meletus, answer. And I must remind the audience of my request that they would not make a disturbance if I speak in my accustomed manner:

Did ever man, Meletus, believe in the existence of human things, and not of human beings?...I wish, men of Athens, that he would answer, and not be always trying to get up an interruption. Did ever any man believe in horsemanship, and not in horses? or in flute-playing, and not in flute- players? No, my friend; I will answer to you and to the court, as you refuse to answer for yourself. There is no man who ever did. But now please to answer the next question: Can a man believe in spiritual and divine agencies, and not in spirits or demigods?

He cannot.

How lucky I am to have extracted that answer, by the assistance of the court! But then you swear in the indictment that I teach and believe in divine or spiritual agencies (new or old, no matter for that); at any rate, I believe in spiritual agencies,--so you say and swear in the affidavit; and yet if I believe in divine beings, how can I help believing in spirits or demigods;--must I not? To be sure I must; and therefore I may assume that your silence gives consent. Now what are spirits or demigods? Are they not either gods or the sons of gods?

Certainly they are.

But this is what I call the facetious riddle invented by you: the demigods or spirits are gods, and you say first that I do not believe in gods, and then again that I do believe in gods; that is, if I believe in demigods. For if the demigods are the illegitimate sons of gods, whether by the nymphs or by any other mothers, of whom they are said to be the sons--what human being will ever believe that there are no gods if they are the sons of gods? You might as well affirm the existence of mules, and deny that of horses and asses. Such nonsense, Meletus, could only have been intended by you to make trial of me. You have put this into the indictment because you had nothing real of which to accuse me. But no

one who has a particle of understanding will ever be convinced by you that the same men can believe in divine and
superhuman things, and yet not believe that there are gods
and demigods and heroes.

I have said enough in answer to the charge of Meletus:
any elaborate defence is unnecessary, but I know only too
well how many are the enmities which I have incurred, and
this is what will be my destruction if I am destroyed;--not
Meletus, nor yet Anytus, but the envy and detraction of the
world, which has been the death of many good men, and will
probably be the death of many more; there is no danger of my
being the last of them.

Some one will say: And are you not ashamed, Socrates,
of a course of life which is likely to bring you to an untimely
end? To him I may fairly answer: There you are mistaken:
a man who is good for anything ought not to calculate the
chance of living or dying; he ought only to consider whether
in doing anything he is doing right or wrong--acting the part
of a good man or of a bad. Whereas, upon your view, the
heroes who fell at Troy were not good for much, and the son
of Thetis above all, who altogether despised danger in comparison with disgrace; and when he was so eager to slay Hector, his goddess mother said to him, that if he avenged his
companion Patroclus, and slew Hector, he would die himself-
-'Fate,' she said, in these or the like words, 'waits for you next
after Hector;' he, receiving this warning, utterly despised
danger and death, and instead of fearing them, feared rather
to live in dishonour, and not to avenge his friend. 'Let me die
forthwith,' he replies, 'and be avenged of my enemy, rather
than abide here by the beaked ships, a laughing-stock and a
burden of the earth.' Had Achilles any thought of death and
danger? For wherever a man's place is, whether the place
which he has chosen or that in which he has been placed by a
commander, there he ought to remain in the hour of danger;
he should not think of death or of anything but of disgrace.
And this, O men of Athens, is a true saying.

Strange, indeed, would be my conduct, O men of Athens,
if I who, when I was ordered by the generals whom you chose

to command me at Potidaea and Amphipolis and Delium, remained where they placed me, like any other man, facing
death--if now, when, as I conceive and imagine, God orders
me to fulfil the philosopher's mission of searching into myself and other men, I were to desert my post through fear of
death, or any other fear; that would indeed be strange, and I
might justly be arraigned in court for denying the existence
of the gods, if I disobeyed the oracle because I was afraid of
death, fancying that I was wise when I was not wise. For
the fear of death is indeed the pretence of wisdom, and not
real wisdom, being a pretence of knowing the unknown; and
no one knows whether death, which men in their fear apprehend to be the greatest evil, may not be the greatest good. Is
not this ignorance of a disgraceful sort, the ignorance which
is the conceit that a man knows what he does not know? And
in this respect only I believe myself to differ from men in general, and may perhaps claim to be wiser than they are:--that
whereas I know but little of the world below, I do not suppose
that I know: but I do know that injustice and disobedience
to a better, whether God or man, is evil and dishonourable,
and I will never fear or avoid a possible good rather than a
certain evil. And therefore if you let me go now, and are not
convinced by Anytus, who said that since I had been prosecuted I must be put to death; (or if not that I ought never to
have been prosecuted at all); and that if I escape now, your
sons will all be utterly ruined by listening to my words--if
you say to me, Socrates, this time we will not mind Anytus,
and you shall be let off, but upon one condition, that you are
not to enquire and speculate in this way any more, and that
if you are caught doing so again you shall die;--if this was the
condition on which you let me go, I should reply: Men of Athens, I honour and love you; but I shall obey God rather than
you, and while I have life and strength I shall never cease
from the practice and teaching of philosophy, exhorting any
one whom I meet and saying to him after my manner: You,
my friend,--a citizen of the great and mighty and wise city
of Athens,--are you not ashamed of heaping up the greatest
amount of money and honour and reputation, and caring so
little about wisdom and truth and the greatest improvement

of the soul, which you never regard or heed at all? And if the person with whom I am arguing, says: Yes, but I do care; then I do not leave him or let him go at once; but I proceed to interrogate and examine and cross-examine him, and if I think that he has no virtue in him, but only says that he has, I reproach him with undervaluing the greater, and overvaluing the less. And I shall repeat the same words to every one whom I meet, young and old, citizen and alien, but especially to the citizens, inasmuch as they are my brethren. For know that this is the command of God; and I believe that no greater good has ever happened in the state than my service to the God. For I do nothing but go about persuading you all, old and young alike, not to take thought for your persons or your properties, but first and chiefly to care about the greatest improvement of the soul. I tell you that virtue is not given by money, but that from virtue comes money and every other good of man, public as well as private. This is my teaching, and if this is the doctrine which corrupts the youth, I am a mischievous person. But if any one says that this is not my teaching, he is speaking an untruth. Wherefore, O men of Athens, I say to you, do as Anytus bids or not as Anytus bids, and either acquit me or not; but whichever you do, understand that I shall never alter my ways, not even if I have to die many times.

Men of Athens, do not interrupt, but hear me; there was an understanding between us that you should hear me to the end: I have something more to say, at which you may be inclined to cry out; but I believe that to hear me will be good for you, and therefore I beg that you will not cry out. I would have you know, that if you kill such an one as I am, you will injure yourselves more than you will injure me. Nothing will injure me, not Meletus nor yet Anytus--they cannot, for a bad man is not permitted to injure a better than himself. I do not deny that Anytus may, perhaps, kill him, or drive him into exile, or deprive him of civil rights; and he may imagine, and others may imagine, that he is inflicting a great injury upon him: but there I do not agree. For the evil of doing as he is doing--the evil of unjustly taking away the life of another--is greater far.

And now, Athenians, I am not going to argue for my own
sake, as you may think, but for yours, that you may not sin
against the God by condemning me, who am his gift to you.
For if you kill me you will not easily find a successor to me,
who, if I may use such a ludicrous figure of speech, am a sort
of gadfly, given to the state by God; and the state is a great
and noble steed who is tardy in his motions owing to his very
size, and requires to be stirred into life. I am that gadfly
which God has attached to the state, and all day long and
in all places am always fastening upon you, arousing and
persuading and reproaching you. You will not easily find another like me, and therefore I would advise you to spare me.
I dare say that you may feel out of temper (like a person who
is suddenly awakened from sleep), and you think that you
might easily strike me dead as Anytus advises, and then you
would sleep on for the remainder of your lives, unless God in
his care of you sent you another gadfly. When I say that I
am given to you by God, the proof of my mission is this:--if I
had been like other men, I should not have neglected all my
own concerns or patiently seen the neglect of them during
all these years, and have been doing yours, coming to you
individually like a father or elder brother, exhorting you to
regard virtue; such conduct, I say, would be unlike human
nature. If I had gained anything, or if my exhortations had
been paid, there would have been some sense in my doing so;
but now, as you will perceive, not even the impudence of my
accusers dares to say that I have ever exacted or sought pay
of any one; of that they have no witness. And I have a sufficient witness to the truth of what I say--my poverty.

Some one may wonder why I go about in private giving
advice and busying myself with the concerns of others, but do
not venture to come forward in public and advise the state. I
will tell you why. You have heard me speak at sundry times
and in divers places of an oracle or sign which comes to me,
and is the divinity which Meletus ridicules in the indictment.
This sign, which is a kind of voice, first began to come to me
when I was a child; it always forbids but never commands me
to do anything which I am going to do. This is what deters
me from being a politician. And rightly, as I think. For I am

certain, O men of Athens, that if I had engaged in politics, I should have perished long ago, and done no good either to you or to myself. And do not be offended at my telling you the truth: for the truth is, that no man who goes to war with you or any other multitude, honestly striving against the many lawless and unrighteous deeds which are done in a state, will save his life; he who will fight for the right, if he would live even for a brief space, must have a private station and not a public one.

I can give you convincing evidence of what I say, not words only, but what you value far more--actions. Let me relate to you a passage of my own life which will prove to you that I should never have yielded to injustice from any fear of death, and that 'as I should have refused to yield' I must have died at once. I will tell you a tale of the courts, not very interesting perhaps, but nevertheless true. The only office of state which I ever held, O men of Athens, was that of senator: the tribe Antiochis, which is my tribe, had the presidency at the trial of the generals who had not taken up the bodies of the slain after the battle of Arginusae; and you proposed to try them in a body, contrary to law, as you all thought afterwards; but at the time I was the only one of the Prytanes who was opposed to the illegality, and I gave my vote against you; and when the orators threatened to impeach and arrest me, and you called and shouted, I made up my mind that I would run the risk, having law and justice with me, rather than take part in your injustice because I feared imprisonment and death. This happened in the days of the democracy. But when the oligarchy of the Thirty was in power, they sent for me and four others into the rotunda, and bade us bring Leon the Salaminian from Salamis, as they wanted to put him to death. This was a specimen of the sort of commands which they were always giving with the view of implicating as many as possible in their crimes; and then I showed, not in word only but in deed, that, if I may be allowed to use such an expression, I cared not a straw for death, and that my great and only care was lest I should do an unrighteous or unholy thing. For the strong arm of that oppressive power did not frighten me into doing wrong; and when we came out of the rotunda the other four went to Salamis and fetched Leon, but I went quietly home. For which I might have lost my life, had not the power of the Thirty shortly afterwards come to an end. And many will witness to my words.

Now do you really imagine that I could have survived all these years, if I had led a public life, supposing that like a good man I had always maintained the right and had made justice, as I ought, the first thing? No indeed, men of Athens, neither I nor any other man. But I have been always the same in all my actions, public as well as private, and never have I yielded any base compliance to those who are slanderously termed my disciples, or to any other. Not that I have any regular disciples. But if any one likes to come and hear me while I am pursuing my mission, whether he be young or old, he is not excluded. Nor do I converse only with those who pay; but any one, whether he be rich or poor, may ask and answer me and listen to my words; and whether he turns out to be a bad man or a good one, neither result can be justly imputed to me; for I never taught or professed to teach him anything. And if any one says that he has ever learned or heard anything from me in private which all the world has not heard, let me tell you that he is lying.

But I shall be asked, Why do people delight in continually conversing with you? I have told you already, Athenians, the whole truth about this matter: they like to hear the cross-examination of the pretenders to wisdom; there is amusement in it. Now this duty of cross-examining other men has been imposed upon me by God; and has been signified to me by oracles, visions, and in every way in which the will of divine power was ever intimated to any one. This is true, O Athenians, or, if not true, would be soon refuted. If I am or have been corrupting the youth, those of them who are now grown up and have become sensible that I gave them bad advice in the days of their youth should come forward as accusers, and take their revenge; or if they do not like to come themselves, some of their relatives, fathers, brothers, or other kinsmen, should say what evil their families have suffered at my hands. Now is their time. Many of them I see in the court. There is Crito, who is of the same age and of the same deme with myself, and there is Critobulus his son, whom I also see. Then again there is Lysanias of Sphettus, who is the father of Aeschines--he is present; and also there is Antiphon of Cephisus, who is the father of Epigenes; and there are the brothers of several who have associated with me. There is Nicostratus the son of Theosdotides, and the brother of Theodotus (now Theodotus himself is dead, and therefore he, at any rate, will not seek to stop him); and there is Paralus the son of Demodocus, who had a brother Theages; and Adeimantus the son of Ariston, whose brother Plato is present; and Aeantodorus, who is the brother of Apollodorus, whom I also see. I might mention a great many others, some of whom Meletus should have produced as witnesses in the course of his speech; and let him still produce them, if he has forgotten--I will make way for him. And let him say, if he has any testimony of the sort which he can produce. Nay, Athenians, the very opposite is the truth. For all these are ready to witness on behalf of the corrupter, of the injurer of their kindred, as Meletus and Anytus call me; not the cor- rupted youth only--there might have been a motive for that- -but their uncorrupted elder relatives. Why should they too support me with their testimony? Why, indeed, except for the sake of truth and justice, and because they know that I am speaking the truth, and that Meletus is a liar.

Well, Athenians, this and the like of this is all the defence which I have to offer. Yet a word more. Perhaps there may be some one who is offended at me, when he calls to mind how he himself on a similar, or even a less serious occasion, prayed and entreated the judges with many tears, and how he produced his children in court, which was a moving spec- tacle, together with a host of relations and friends; whereas I, who am probably in danger of my life, will do none of these things. The contrast may occur to his mind, and he may be set against me, and vote in anger because he is displeased at me on this account. Now if there be such a person among you,--mind, I do not say that there is,--to him I may fairly reply: My friend, I am a man, and like other men, a crea- ture of flesh and blood, and not 'of wood or stone,' as Homer

says; and I have a family, yes, and sons, O Athenians, three
in number, one almost a man, and two others who are still
young; and yet I will not bring any of them hither in order
to petition you for an acquittal. And why not? Not from any
self-assertion or want of respect for you. Whether I am or
am not afraid of death is another question, of which I will
not now speak. But, having regard to public opinion, I feel
that such conduct would be discreditable to myself, and to
you, and to the whole state. One who has reached my years,
and who has a name for wisdom, ought not to demean himself. Whether this opinion of me be deserved or not, at any
rate the world has decided that Socrates is in some way superior to other men. And if those among you who are said
to be superior in wisdom and courage, and any other virtue,
demean themselves in this way, how shameful is their conduct! I have seen men of reputation, when they have been
condemned, behaving in the strangest manner: they seemed
to fancy that they were going to suffer something dreadful
if they died, and that they could be immortal if you only allowed them to live; and I think that such are a dishonour
to the state, and that any stranger coming in would have
said of them that the most eminent men of Athens, to whom
the Athenians themselves give honour and command, are no
better than women. And I say that these things ought not
to be done by those of us who have a reputation; and if they
are done, you ought not to permit them; you ought rather to
show that you are far more disposed to condemn the man
who gets up a doleful scene and makes the city ridiculous,
than him who holds his peace.

But, setting aside the question of public opinion, there
seems to be something wrong in asking a favour of a judge,
and thus procuring an acquittal, instead of informing and
convincing him. For his duty is, not to make a present of
justice, but to give judgment; and he has sworn that he will
judge according to the laws, and not according to his own good
pleasure; and we ought not to encourage you, nor should you
allow yourselves to be encouraged, in this habit of perjury-
-there can be no piety in that. Do not then require me to
do what I consider dishonourable and impious and wrong,

especially now, when I am being tried for impiety on the indictment of Meletus. For if, O men of Athens, by force of
persuasion and entreaty I could overpower your oaths, then I
should be teaching you to believe that there are no gods, and
in defending should simply convict myself of the charge of
not believing in them. But that is not so--far otherwise. For
I do believe that there are gods, and in a sense higher than
that in which any of my accusers believe in them. And to you
and to God I commit my cause, to be determined by you as is
best for you and me.

...

There are many reasons why I am not grieved, O men of
Athens, at the vote of condemnation. I expected it, and am
only surprised that the votes are so nearly equal; for I had
thought that the majority against me would have been far
larger; but now, had thirty votes gone over to the other side,
I should have been acquitted. And I may say, I think, that I
have escaped Meletus. I may say more; for without the assistance of Anytus and Lycon, any one may see that he would
not have had a fifth part of the votes, as the law requires,
in which case he would have incurred a fine of a thousand
drachmae.

And so he proposes death as the penalty. And what shall
I propose on my part, O men of Athens? Clearly that which
is my due. And what is my due? What return shall be made
to the man who has never had the wit to be idle during his
whole life; but has been careless of what the many care for--
wealth, and family interests, and military offices, and speaking in the assembly, and magistracies, and plots, and parties.
Reflecting that I was really too honest a man to be a politician and live, I did not go where I could do no good to you or
to myself; but where I could do the greatest good privately to
every one of you, thither I went, and sought to persuade every man among you that he must look to himself, and seek virtue and wisdom before he looks to his private interests, and
look to the state before he looks to the interests of the state;
and that this should be the order which he observes in all his
actions. What shall be done to such an one? Doubtless some

good thing, O men of Athens, if he has his reward; and the good should be of a kind suitable to him. What would be a reward suitable to a poor man who is your benefactor, and who desires leisure that he may instruct you? There can be no reward so fitting as maintenance in the Prytaneum, O men of Athens, a reward which he deserves far more than the citizen who has won the prize at Olympia in the horse or chariot race, whether the chariots were drawn by two horses or by many. For I am in want, and he has enough; and he only gives you the appearance of happiness, and I give you the reality. And if I am to estimate the penalty fairly, I should say that maintenance in the Prytaneum is the just return.

Perhaps you think that I am braving you in what I am saying now, as in what I said before about the tears and prayers. But this is not so. I speak rather because I am convinced that I never intentionally wronged any one, although I cannot convince you--the time has been too short; if there were a law at Athens, as there is in other cities, that a capital cause should not be decided in one day, then I believe that I should have convinced you. But I cannot in a moment refute great slanders; and, as I am convinced that I never wronged another, I will assuredly not wrong myself. I will not say of myself that I deserve any evil, or propose any penalty. Why should I? because I am afraid of the penalty of death which Meletus proposes? When I do not know whether death is a good or an evil, why should I propose a penalty which would certainly be an evil? Shall I say imprisonment? And why should I live in prison, and be the slave of the magistrates of the year--of the Eleven? Or shall the penalty be a fine, and imprisonment until the fine is paid? There is the same objection. I should have to lie in prison, for money I have none, and cannot pay. And if I say exile (and this may possibly be the penalty which you will affix), I must indeed be blinded by the love of life, if I am so irrational as to expect that when you, who are my own citizens, cannot endure my discourses and words, and have found them so grievous and odious that you will have no more of them, others are likely to endure me. No indeed, men of Athens, that is not very likely. And what a life should I lead, at my age, wandering from city to city, ever changing my place of exile, and always being driven out! For I am quite sure that wherever I go, there, as here, the young men will flock to me; and if I drive them away, their elders will drive me out at their request; and if I let them come, their fathers and friends will drive me out for their sakes.

Some one will say: Yes, Socrates, but cannot you hold your tongue, and then you may go into a foreign city, and no one will interfere with you? Now I have great difficulty in making you understand my answer to this. For if I tell you that to do as you say would be a disobedience to the God, and therefore that I cannot hold my tongue, you will not believe that I am serious; and if I say again that daily to discourse about virtue, and of those other things about which you hear me examining myself and others, is the greatest good of man, and that the unexamined life is not worth living, you are still less likely to believe me. Yet I say what is true, although a thing of which it is hard for me to persuade you. Also, I have never been accustomed to think that I deserve to suffer any harm. Had I money I might have estimated the offence at what I was able to pay, and not have been much the worse. But I have none, and therefore I must ask you to proportion the fine to my means. Well, perhaps I could afford a mina, and therefore I propose that penalty: Plato, Crito, Critobulus, and Apollodorus, my friends here, bid me say thirty minae, and they will be the sureties. Let thirty minae be the penalty; for which sum they will be ample security to you.

...

Not much time will be gained, O Athenians, in return for the evil name which you will get from the detractors of the city, who will say that you killed Socrates, a wise man; for they will call me wise, even although I am not wise, when they want to reproach you. If you had waited a little while, your desire would have been fulfilled in the course of nature. For I am far advanced in years, as you may perceive, and not far from death. I am speaking now not to all of you, but only to those who have condemned me to death. And I have another thing to say to them: you think that I was convicted because I had no words of the sort which would have procured my acquittal--I mean, if I had thought fit to leave nothing undone or unsaid. Not so; the deficiency which led to my conviction was not of words-- certainly not. But I had not the boldness or impudence or inclination to address you as you would have liked me to do, weeping and wailing and lamenting, and saying and doing many things which you have been accustomed to hear from others, and which, as I maintain, are unworthy of me. I thought at the time that I ought not to do anything common or mean when in danger: nor do I now repent of the style of my defence; I would rather die having spoken after my manner, than speak in your manner and live. For neither in war nor yet at law ought I or any man to use every way of escaping death. Often in battle there can be no doubt that if a man will throw away his arms, and fall on his knees before his pursuers, he may escape death; and in other dangers there are other ways of escaping death, if a man is willing to say and do anything. The difficulty, my friends, is not to avoid death, but to avoid unrighteousness; for that runs faster than death. I am old and move slowly, and the slower runner has overtaken me, and my accusers are keen and quick, and the faster runner, who is unrighteousness, has overtaken them. And now I depart hence condemned by you to suffer the penalty of death,--they too go their ways condemned by the truth to suffer the penalty of villainy and wrong; and I must abide by my award--let them abide by theirs. I suppose that these things may be regarded as fated,--and I think that they are well.

And now, O men who have condemned me, I would fain prophesy to you; for I am about to die, and in the hour of death men are gifted with prophetic power. And I prophesy to you who are my murderers, that immediately after my departure punishment far heavier than you have inflicted on me will surely await you. Me you have killed because you wanted to escape the accuser, and not to give an account of your lives. But that will not be as you suppose: far otherwise. For I say that there will be more accusers of you than there are now; accusers whom hitherto I have restrained: and as they are younger they will be more inconsiderate with you, and you will be more offended at them. If you think that by killing men you can prevent some one from censuring your evil lives, you are mistaken; that is not a way of escape which is either possible or honourable; the easiest and the noblest way is not to be disabling others, but to be improving yourselves. This is the prophecy which I utter before my departure to the judges who have condemned me.

Friends, who would have acquitted me, I would like also to talk with you about the thing which has come to pass, while the magistrates are busy, and before I go to the place at which I must die. Stay then a little, for we may as well talk with one another while there is time. You are my friends, and I should like to show you the meaning of this event which has happened to me. O my judges--for you I may truly call judges--I should like to tell you of a wonderful circumstance. Hitherto the divine faculty of which the internal oracle is the source has constantly been in the habit of opposing me even about trifles, if I was going to make a slip or error in any matter; and now as you see there has come upon me that which may be thought, and is generally believed to be, the last and worst evil. But the oracle made no sign of opposition, either when I was leaving my house in the morning, or when I was on my way to the court, or while I was speaking, at anything which I was going to say; and yet I have often been stopped in the middle of a speech, but now in nothing I either said or did touching the matter in hand has the oracle opposed me. What do I take to be the explanation of this silence? I will tell you. It is an intimation that what has happened to me is a good, and that those of us who think that death is an evil are in error. For the customary sign would surely have opposed me had I been going to evil and not to good.

Let us reflect in another way, and we shall see that there is great reason to hope that death is a good; for one of two things--either death is a state of nothingness and utter unconsciousness, or, as men say, there is a change and migration of the soul from this world to another. Now if you suppose that there is no consciousness, but a sleep like the sleep of him who is undisturbed even by dreams, death will be an

unspeakable gain. For if a person were to select the night in
which his sleep was undisturbed even by dreams, and were
to compare with this the other days and nights of his life,
and then were to tell us how many days and nights he had
passed in the course of his life better and more pleasantly
than this one, I think that any man, I will not say a private
man, but even the great king will not find many such days
or nights, when compared with the others. Now if death be
of such a nature, I say that to die is gain; for eternity is then
only a single night. But if death is the journey to another
place, and there, as men say, all the dead abide, what good,
O my friends and judges, can be greater than this? If indeed
when the pilgrim arrives in the world below, he is delivered
from the professors of justice in this world, and finds the true
judges who are said to give judgment there, Minos and Rh-
adamanthus and Aeacus and Triptolemus, and other sons
of God who were righteous in their own life, that pilgrimage will be worth making. What would not a man give if he
might converse with Orpheus and Musaeus and Hesiod and
Homer? Nay, if this be true, let me die again and again. I
myself, too, shall have a wonderful interest in there meeting
and conversing with Palamedes, and Ajax the son of Telamon,
and any other ancient hero who has suffered death through
an unjust judgment; and there will be no small pleasure, as
I think, in comparing my own sufferings with theirs. Above
all, I shall then be able to continue my search into true and
false knowledge; as in this world, so also in the next; and I
shall find out who is wise, and who pretends to be wise, and
is not. What would not a man give, O judges, to be able to
examine the leader of the great Trojan expedition; or Odysseus or Sisyphus, or numberless others, men and women too!
What infinite delight would there be in conversing with them
and asking them questions! In another world they do not
put a man to death for asking questions: assuredly not. For
besides being happier than we are, they will be immortal, if
what is said is true.

Wherefore, O judges, be of good cheer about death, and
know of a certainty, that no evil can happen to a good man,
either in life or after death. He and his are not neglected

by the gods; nor has my own approaching end happened by mere chance. But I see clearly that the time had arrived when it was better for me to die and be released from trouble; wherefore the oracle gave no sign. For which reason, also, I am not angry with my condemners, or with my accusers; they have done me no harm, although they did not mean to do me any good; and for this I may gently blame them.

Still I have a favour to ask of them. When my sons are grown up, I would ask you, O my friends, to punish them; and I would have you trouble them, as I have troubled you, if they seem to care about riches, or anything, more than about virtue; or if they pretend to be something when they are really nothing,--then reprove them, as I have reproved you, for not caring about that for which they ought to care, and thinking that they are something when they are really nothing. And if you do this, both I and my sons will have received justice at your hands.

The hour of departure has arrived, and we go our ways--I to die, and you to live. Which is better God only knows.

III.

Crito

PERSONS OF THE DIALOGUE

SOCRATES

CRITO

SCENE: The Prison of Socrates

Socrates. WHY have you come at this hour, Crito? it must be quite early.

Crito. Yes, certainly.

Soc. What is the exact time?

Cr. The dawn is breaking.

Soc. I wonder the keeper of the prison would let you in.

Cr. He knows me because I often come, Socrates; moreover. I have done him a kindness.

Soc. And are you only just come?

Cr. No, I came some time ago.

Soc. Then why did you sit and say nothing, instead of awakening me at once?

Cr. Why, indeed, Socrates, I myself would rather not have all this sleeplessness and sorrow. But I have been wondering at your peaceful slumbers, and that was the reason why I did not awaken you, because I wanted you to be out of pain. I have always thought you happy in the calmness of your temperament; but never did I see the like of the easy, cheerful way in which you bear this calamity.

Soc. Why, Crito, when a man has reached my age he ought not to be repining at the prospect of death.

Cr. And yet other old men find themselves in similar misfortunes, and age does not prevent them from repining.

Soc. That may be. But you have not told me why you come at this early hour.

Cr. I come to bring you a message which is sad and painful; not, as I believe, to yourself but to all of us who are your friends, and saddest of all to me.

Soc. What! I suppose that the ship has come from Delos,

on the arrival of which I am to die?

Cr. No, the ship has not actually arrived, but she will probably be here to-day, as persons who have come from Sunium tell me that they have left her there; and therefore to-morrow, Socrates, will be the last day of your life.

Soc. Very well, Crito; if such is the will of God, I am willing; but my belief is that there will be a delay of a day.

Cr. Why do you say this?

Soc. I will tell you. I am to die on the day after the arrival of the ship?

Cr. Yes; that is what the authorities say.

Soc. But I do not think that the ship will be here until to-morrow; this I gather from a vision which I had last night, or rather only just now, when you fortunately allowed me to sleep.

Cr. And what was the nature of the vision?

Soc. There came to me the likeness of a woman, fair and comely, clothed in white raiment, who called to me and said: O Socrates-

"The third day hence, to Phthia shalt thou go."

Cr. What a singular dream, Socrates!

Soc. There can be no doubt about the meaning Crito, I think.

Cr. Yes: the meaning is only too clear. But, O! my beloved Socrates, let me entreat you once more to take my advice and escape. For if you die I shall not only lose a friend who can never be replaced, but there is another evil: people who do not know you and me will believe that I might have saved you if I had been willing to give money, but that I did not care. Now, can there be a worse disgrace than this- that I should be thought to value money more than the life of a friend? For the many will not be persuaded that I wanted you to escape, and that you refused.

Soc. But why, my dear Crito, should we care about the opinion of the many? Good men, and they are the only persons who are worth considering, will think of these things truly as they happened.

Cr. But do you see. Socrates, that the opinion of the many must be regarded, as is evident in your own case, because they can do the very greatest evil to anyone who has lost their good opinion?

Soc. I only wish, Crito, that they could; for then they could also do the greatest good, and that would be well. But the truth is, that they can do neither good nor evil: they cannot make a man wise or make him foolish; and whatever they do is the result of chance.

Cr. Well, I will not dispute about that; but please to tell me, Socrates, whether you are not acting out of regard to me and your other friends: are you not afraid that if you escape hence we may get into trouble with the informers for having stolen you away, and lose either the whole or a great part of our property; or that even a worse evil may happen to us? Now, if this is your fear, be at ease; for in order to save you, we ought surely to run this or even a greater risk; be persuaded, then, and do as I say.

Soc. Yes, Crito, that is one fear which you mention, but by no means the only one.

Cr. Fear not. There are persons who at no great cost are willing to save you and bring you out of prison; and as for the informers, you may observe that they are far from being exorbitant in their demands; a little money will satisfy them. My means, which, as I am sure, are ample, are at your service, and if you have a scruple about spending all mine, here are strangers who will give you the use of theirs; and one of them, Simmias the Theban, has brought a sum of money for this very purpose; and Cebes and many others are willing to spend their money too. I say, therefore, do not on that account hesitate about making your escape, and do not say, as you did in the court, that you will have a difficulty in knowing what to do with yourself if you escape. For men will love you in other places to which you may go, and not in Athens only; there are friends of mine in Thessaly, if you like to go to them, who will value and protect you, and no Thessalian will give you any trouble. Nor can I think that you are justified, Socrates, in betraying your own life when you might be saved; this is playing into the hands of your enemies and destroyers; and moreover I should say that you were betraying your children; for you might bring them up and educate them; instead of which you go away and leave them, and they will have to take their chance; and if they do not meet with the usual fate of orphans, there will be small thanks to you. No man should bring children into the world who is unwilling to persevere to the end in their nurture and education. But you are choosing the easier part, as I think, not the better and manlier, which would rather have become one who professes virtue in all his actions, like yourself. And, indeed, I am ashamed not only of you, but of us who are your friends, when I reflect that this entire business of yours will be attributed to our want of courage. The trial need never have come on, or might have been brought to another issue; and the end of all, which is the crowning absurdity, will seem to have been permitted by us, through cowardice and baseness, who might have saved you, as you might have saved yourself, if we had been good for anything (for there was no difficulty in escaping); and we did not see how disgraceful, Socrates, and also miserable all this will be to us as well as to you. Make your mind up then, or rather have your mind already made up, for the time of deliberation is over, and there is only one thing to be done, which must be done, if at all, this very night, and which any delay will render all but impossible; I beseech you therefore, Socrates, to be persuaded by me, and to do as I say.

Soc. Dear Crito, your zeal is invaluable, if a right one; but if wrong, the greater the zeal the greater the evil; and therefore we ought to consider whether these things shall be done or not. For I am and always have been one of those natures who must be guided by reason, whatever the reason

may be which upon reflection appears to me to be the best;
and now that this fortune has come upon me, I cannot put
away the reasons which I have before given: the principles
which I have hitherto honored and revered I still honor, and
unless we can find other and better principles on the instant,
I am certain not to agree with you; no, not even if the power of the multitude could inflict many more imprisonments,
confiscations, deaths, frightening us like children with hobgoblin terrors. But what will be the fairest way of considering the question? Shall I return to your old argument about
the opinions of men, some of which are to be regarded, and
others, as we were saying, are not to be regarded? Now were
we right in maintaining this before I was condemned? And
has the argument which was once good now proved to be talk
for the sake of talking; in fact an amusement only, and altogether vanity? That is what I want to consider with your
help, Crito: whether, under my present circumstances, the
argument appears to be in any way different or not; and is
to be allowed by me or disallowed. That argument, which, as
I believe, is maintained by many who assume to be authorities, was to the effect, as I was saying, that the opinions of
some men are to be regarded, and of other men not to be
regarded. Now you, Crito, are a disinterested person who are
not going to die to-morrow- at least, there is no human probability of this, and you are therefore not liable to be deceived
by the circumstances in which you are placed. Tell me, then,
whether I am right in saying that some opinions, and the
opinions of some men only, are to be valued, and other opinions, and the opinions of other men, are not to be valued. I
ask you whether I was right in maintaining this?

Cr. Certainly.

Soc. The good are to be regarded, and not the bad?

Cr. Yes.

Soc. And the opinions of the wise are good, and the opinions of the unwise are evil?

Cr. Certainly.

Soc. And what was said about another matter? Was the disciple in gymnastics supposed to attend to the praise and blame and opinion of every man, or of one man only- his physician or trainer, whoever that was?

Cr. Of one man only.

Soc. And he ought to fear the censure and welcome the praise of that one only, and not of the many?

Cr. That is clear.

Soc. And he ought to live and train, and eat and drink in the way which seems good to his single master who has understanding, rather than according to the opinion of all other men put together?

Cr. True.

Soc. And if he disobeys and disregards the opinion and approval of the one, and regards the opinion of the many who have no understanding, will he not suffer evil?

Cr. Certainly he will.

Soc. And what will the evil be, whither tending and what affcting, in the disobedient person?

Cr. Clearly, affecting the body; that is what is destroyed by the evil.

Soc. Very good; and is not this true, Crito, of other things which we need not separately enumerate? In the matter of just and unjust, fair and foul, good and evil, which are the subjects of our present consultation, ought we to follow the opinion of the many and to fear them; or the opinion of the one man who has understanding, and whom we ought to fear and reverence more than all the rest of the world: and whom deserting we shall destroy and injure that principle in us which may be assumed to be improved by justice and deteriorated by injustice; is there not such a principle?

Cr. Certainly there is, Socrates.

Soc. Take a parallel instance; if, acting under the advice of men who have no understanding, we destroy that which is improvable by health and deteriorated by disease- when that has been destroyed, I say, would life be worth having? And that is- the body?

Cr. Yes.

Soc. Could we live, having an evil and corrupted body?

Cr. Certainly not.

Soc. And will life be worth having, if that higher part of man be depraved, which is improved by justice and deteriorated by injustice? Do we suppose that principle, whatever it may be in man, which has to do with justice and injustice, to be inferior to the body?

Cr. Certainly not.

Soc. More honored, then?

Cr. Far more honored.

Soc. Then, my friend, we must not regard what the many say of us: but what he, the one man who has understanding of just and unjust, will say, and what the truth will say. And therefore you begin in error when you suggest that we should regard the opinion of the many about just and unjust, good and evil, honorable and dishonorable. Well, someone will say, "But the many can kill us."

Cr. Yes, Socrates; that will clearly be the answer.

Soc. That is true; but still I find with surprise that the old argument is, as I conceive, unshaken as ever. And I should like to know Whether I may say the same of another proposition- that not life, but a good life, is to be chiefly valued?

Cr. Yes, that also remains.

Soc. And a good life is equivalent to a just and honorable one- that holds also?

Cr. Yes, that holds.

Soc. From these premises I proceed to argue the question whether I ought or ought not to try to escape without the consent of the Athenians: and if I am clearly right in escaping, then I will make the attempt; but if not, I will abstain. The other considerations which you mention, of money and loss of character, and the duty of educating children, are, I fear, only the doctrines of the multitude, who would be as ready to call people to life, if they were able, as they are to put them to death- and with as little reason. But now, since the argument has thus far prevailed, the only question which remains to be considered is, whether we shall do rightly either in escaping or in suffering others to aid in our escape and paying them in money and thanks, or whether we shan not do rightly; and if the latter, then death or any other calamity which may ensue on my remaining here must not be allowed to enter into the calculation.

Cr. I think that you are right, Socrates; how then shall we proceed?

Soc. Let us consider the matter together, and do you either refute me if you can, and I will be convinced; or else cease, my dear friend, from repeating to me that I ought to escape against the wishes of the Athenians: for I am extremely desirous to be persuaded by you, but not against my own better judgment. And now please to consider my first position, and do your best to answer me.

Cr. I will do my best.

Soc. Are we to say that we are never intentionally to do wrong, or that in one way we ought and in another way we ought not to do wrong, or is doing wrong always evil and dishonorable, as I was just now saying, and as has been already acknowledged by us? Are all our former admissions which were made within a few days to be thrown away? And have we, at our age, been earnestly discoursing with one another all our life long only to discover that we are no better than children? Or are we to rest assured, in spite of the opinion of the many, and in spite of consequences whether better or worse, of the truth of what was then said, that injustice is always an evil and dishonor to him who acts unjustly? Shall we affirm that?

Cr. Yes.

Soc. Then we must do no wrong?

Cr. Certainly not.

Soc. Nor when injured injure in return, as the many imagine; for we must injure no one at all?

Cr. Clearly not.

Soc. Again, Crito, may we do evil?

Cr. Surely not, Socrates.

Soc. And what of doing evil in return for evil, which is the morality of the many-is that just or not?

Cr. Not just.

Soc. For doing evil to another is the same as injuring him?

Cr. Very true.

Soc. Then we ought not to retaliate or render evil for evil to anyone, whatever evil we may have suffered from him. But I would have you consider, Crito, whether you really mean what you are saying. For this opinion has never been held, and never will be held, by any considerable number of persons; and those who are agreed and those who are not agreed upon this point have no common ground, and can only despise one another, when they see how widely they differ. Tell me, then, whether you agree with and assent to my first principle, that neither injury nor retaliation nor warding off evil by evil is ever right. And shall that be the premise of our agreement? Or do you decline and dissent from this? For this has been of old and is still my opinion; but, if you are of another opinion, let me hear what you have to say. If, however, you remain of the same mind as formerly, I will proceed to the next step.

Cr. You may proceed, for I have not changed my mind.

Soc. Then I will proceed to the next step, which may be put in the form of a question: Ought a man to do what he admits to be right, or ought he to betray the right?

Cr. He ought to do what he thinks right.

Soc. But if this is true, what is the application? In leaving the prison against the will of the Athenians, do I wrong any? or rather do I not wrong those whom I ought least to wrong? Do I not desert the principles which were acknowledged by us to be just? What do you say?

Cr. I cannot tell, Socrates, for I do not know.

Soc. Then consider the matter in this way: Imagine that I am about to play truant (you may call the proceeding by any name which you like), and the laws and the government come and interrogate me: "Tell us, Socrates," they say; "what are you about? are you going by an act of yours to overturn us- the laws and the whole State, as far as in you lies? Do you imagine that a State can subsist and not be overthrown, in which the decisions of law have no power, but are set aside and overthrown by individuals?" What will be our answer, Crito, to these and the like words? Anyone, and especially a clever rhetorician, will have a good deal to urge about the evil of setting aside the law which requires a sentence to be carried out; and we might reply, "Yes; but the State has injured us and given an unjust sentence." Suppose I say that?

Cr. Very good, Socrates.

Soc. "And was that our agreement with you?" the law would sar, "or were you to abide by the sentence of the State?" And if I were to express astonishment at their saying this, the law would probably add: "Answer, Socrates, instead of opening your eyes: you are in the habit of asking and answering questions. Tell us what complaint you have to make against us which justifies you in attempting to destroy us and the State? In the first place did we not bring you into existence? Your father married your mother by our aid and begat you.

Say whether you have any objection to urge against those of us who regulate marriage?" None, I should reply. "Or against those of us who regulate the system of nurture and education of children in which you were trained? Were not the laws, who have the charge of this, right in commanding your father to train you in music and gymnastic?" Right, I should reply. "Well, then, since you were brought into the world and nurtured and educated by us, can you deny in the first place that you are our child and slave, as your fathers were before you? And if this is true you are not on equal terms with us; nor can you think that you have a right to do to us what we are doing to you. Would you have any right to strike or revile or do any other evil to a father or to your master, if you had one, when you have been struck or reviled by him, or received some other evil at his hands?- you would not say this? And because we think right to destroy you, do you think that you have any right to destroy us in return, and your country as far as in you lies? And will you, O professor of true virtue, say that you are justified in this? Has a philosopher like you failed to discover that our country is more to be valued and higher and holier far than mother or father or any ancestor, and more to be regarded in the eyes of the gods and of men of understanding? also to be soothed, and gently and reverently entreated when angry, even more than a father, and if not persuaded, obeyed? And when we are punished by her, whether with imprisonment or stripes, the punishment is to be endured in silence; and if she leads us to wounds or death in battle, thither we follow as is right; neither may anyone yield or retreat or leave his rank, but whether in battle or in a court of law, or in any other place, he must do what his city and his country order him; or he must change their view of what is just: and if he may do no violence to his father or mother, much less may he do violence to his country." What answer shall we make to this, Crito? Do the laws speak truly, or do they not?

Cr. I think that they do.

Soc. Then the laws will say: "Consider, Socrates, if this is true, that in your present attempt you are going to do us wrong. For, after having brought you into the world, and nurtured and educated you, and given you and every other citizen a share in every good that we had to give, we further proclaim and give the right to every Athenian, that if he does not like us when he has come of age and has seen the ways of the city, and made our acquaintance, he may go where he pleases and take his goods with him; and none of us laws will forbid him or interfere with him. Any of you who does not like us and the city, and who wants to go to a colony or to any other city, may go where he likes, and take his goods with him. But he who has experience of the manner in which we order justice and administer the State, and still remains, has entered into an implied contract that he will do as we command him. And he who disobeys us is, as we maintain, thrice wrong: first, because in disobeying us he is disobeying his parents; secondly, because we are the authors of his education; thirdly, because he has made an agreement with us that he will duly obey our commands; and he neither obeys them nor convinces us that our commands are wrong; and we do not rudely impose them, but give him the alternative of obeying or convincing us; that is what we offer and he does neither. These are the sort of accusations to which, as we were saying, you, Socrates, will be exposed if you accomplish your intentions; you, above all other Athenians." Suppose I ask, why is this? they will justly retort upon me that I above all other men have acknowledged the agreement. "There is clear proof," they will say, "Socrates, that we and the city were not displeasing to you. Of all Athenians you have been the most constant resident in the city, which, as you never leave, you may be supposed to love. For you never went out of the city either to see the games, except once when you went to the Isthmus, or to any other place unless when you were on military service; nor did you travel as other men do. Nor had you any curiosity to know other States or their laws: your affections did not go beyond us and our State; we were your especial favorites, and you acquiesced in our government of you; and this is the State in which you begat your children, which is a proof of your satisfaction. Moreover, you might, if you had liked, have fixed the penalty at banishment in the course of the trial-the State which refuses to let you go now would have let you go then. But you pretended that you preferred death to exile, and that you were not grieved at death. And now you have forgotten these fine sentiments, and pay no respect to us, the laws, of whom you are the destroyer; and are doing what only a miserable slave would do, running away and turning your back upon the compacts and agreements which you made as a citizen. And first of all answer this very question: Are we right in saying that you agreed to be governed according to us in deed, and not in word only? Is that true or not?" How shall we answer that, Crito? Must we not agree?

Cr. There is no help, Socrates.

Soc. Then will they not say: "You, Socrates, are breaking the covenants and agreements which you made with us at your leisure, not in any haste or under any compulsion or deception, but having had seventy years to think of them, during which time you were at liberty to leave the city, if we were not to your mind, or if our covenants appeared to you to be unfair. You had your choice, and might have gone either to Lacedaemon or Crete, which you often praise for their good government, or to some other Hellenic or foreign State. Whereas you, above all other Athenians, seemed to be so fond of the State, or, in other words, of us her laws (for who would like a State that has no laws?), that you never stirred out of her: the halt, the blind, the maimed, were not more stationary in her than you were. And now you run away and forsake your agreements. Not so, Socrates, if you will take our advice; do not make yourself ridiculous by escaping out of the city.

"For just consider, if you transgress and err in this sort of way, what good will you do, either to yourself or to your friends? That your friends will be driven into exile and deprived of citizenship, or will lose their property, is tolerably certain; and you yourself, if you fly to one of the neighboring cities, as, for example, Thebes or Megara, both of which are well-governed cities, will come to them as an enemy, Socrates, and their government will be against you, and all patriotic citizens will cast an evil eye upon you as a subverter of the laws, and you will confirm in the minds of the judges the justice of their own condemnation of you. For he who is a corrupter of the laws is more than likely to be corrupter of the young and foolish portion of mankind. Will you then flee from well-ordered cities and virtuous men? and is existence worth having on these terms? Or will you go to them without shame, and talk to them, Socrates? And what will you say to them? What you say here about virtue and justice and institutions and laws being the best things among men? Would that be decent of you? Surely not. But if you go away from well-governed States to Crito's friends in Thessaly, where there is great disorder and license, they will be charmed to have the tale of your escape from prison, set off with ludicrous particulars of the manner in which you were wrapped in a goatskin or some other disguise, and metamorphosed as the fashion of runaways is- that is very likely; but will there be no one to remind you that in your old age you violated the most sacred laws from a miserable desire of a little more life? Perhaps not, if you keep them in a good temper; but if they are out of temper you will hear many degrading things; you will live, but how?- as the flatterer of all men, and the servant of all men; and doing what?- eating and drinking in Thessaly, having gone abroad in order that you may get a dinner. And where will be your fine sentiments about justice and virtue then? Say that you wish to live for the sake of your children, that you may bring them up and educate them- will you take them into Thessaly and deprive them of Athenian citizenship? Is that the benefit which you would confer upon them? Or are you under the impression that they will be better cared for and educated here if you are still alive, although absent from them; for that your friends will take care of them? Do you fancy that if you are an inhabitant of Thessaly they will take care of them, and if you are an inhabitant of the other world they will not take care of them? Nay; but if they who call themselves friends are truly friends, they surely will.

"Listen, then, Socrates, to us who have brought you up. Think not of life and children first, and of justice afterwards, but of justice first, that you may be justified before the princes of the world below. For neither will you nor any that belong to you be happier or holier or juster in this life, or happier in another, if you do as Crito bids. Now you depart in innocence, a sufferer and not a doer of evil; a victim, not of the laws, but of men. But if you go forth, returning evil for evil, and injury for injury, breaking the covenants and agreements which you have made with us, and wronging those whom you ought least to wrong, that is to say, yourself, your friends, your country, and us, we shall be angry with you while you live, and our brethren, the laws in the world below, will receive you as an enemy; for they will know that you have done your best to destroy us. Listen, then, to us and not to Crito."

This is the voice which I seem to hear murmuring in my ears, like the sound of the flute in the ears of the mystic; that voice, I say, is humming in my ears, and prevents me from hearing any other. And I know that anything more which you will say will be in vain. Yet speak, if you have anything to say.

Cr. I have nothing to say, Socrates.

Soc. Then let me follow the intimations of the will of God.

-THE END-

IV.

Meno

PERSONS OF THE DIALOGUE MENO

SOCRATES A SLAVE OF MENO ANYTUS

45/45

Well done
on Summaries

Meno. Can you tell me, Socrates, whether virtue is acquired by teaching or by practice; or if neither by teaching nor practice, then whether it comes to man by nature, or in what other way?

Socrates. O Meno, there was a time when the Thessalians were famous among the other Hellenes only for their riches and their riding; but now, if I am not mistaken, they are equally famous for their wisdom, especially at Larisa, which is the native city of your friend Aristippus. And this is Gorgias' doing; for when he came there, the flower of the Aleuadae, among them your admirer Aristippus, and the other chiefs of the Thessalians, fell in love with his wisdom. And he has taught you the habit of answering questions in a grand and bold style, which becomes those who know, and is the style in which he himself answers all comers; and any Hellene who likes may ask him anything. How different is our lot! my dear Meno. Here at Athens there is a dearth of the commodity, and all wisdom seems to have emigrated from us to you. I am certain that if you were to ask any Athenian whether virtue was natural or acquired, he would laugh in your face, and say: "Stranger, you have far too good an opinion of me, if you think that I can answer your question. For I literally do not know what virtue is, and much less whether it is acquired by teaching or not." And I myself, Meno, living as I do in this region of poverty, am as poor as the rest of the world; and I confess with shame that I know literally nothing about virtue; and when I do not know the "quid" of anything how can I know the "quale"? How, if I knew nothing at all of Meno, could I tell if he was fair, or the opposite of fair; rich and noble, or the reverse of rich and noble? Do you think that I could?

Men. No, Indeed. But are you in earnest, Socrates, in saying that you do not know what virtue is? And am I to carry back this report of you to Thessaly?

Soc. Not only that, my dear boy, but you may say further that I have never known of any one else who did, in my judgment.

Men. Then you have never met Gorgias when he was at Athens?

Soc. Yes, I have.

Men. And did you not think that he knew?

Socrates does not have a good memory

Soc. I have not a good memory, Meno, and therefore I cannot now tell what I thought of him at the time. And I dare say that he did know, and that you know what he said: please, therefore, to remind me of what he said; or, if you would rather, tell me your own view; for I suspect that you and he think much alike.

Men. Very true.

Soc. Then as he is not here, never mind him, and do you tell me: By the gods, Meno, be generous, and tell me what you say that virtue is; for I shall be truly delighted to find that I have been mistaken, and that you and Gorgias do really have this knowledge; although I have been just saying that I have never found anybody who had.

Meno's idea of virtue

Men. There will be no difficulty, Socrates, in answering your question. Let us take first the virtue of a man-he should know how to administer the state, and in the administration of it to benefit his friends and harm his enemies; and he must also be careful not to suffer harm himself. A woman's virtue, if you wish to know about that, may also be easily described: her duty is to order her house, and keep what is indoors, and obey her husband. Every age, every condition of life, young or old, male or female, bond or free, has a different virtue: there are virtues numberless, and no lack of definitions of them; for virtue is relative to the actions and ages of each of us in all that we do. And the same may be said of vice, Socrates.

Soc. How fortunate I am, Meno! When I ask you for one virtue, you present me with a swarm of them, which are in your keeping. Suppose that I carry on the figure of the swarm, and ask of you, What is the nature of the bee? and you answer that there are many kinds of bees, and I reply: But do bees differ as bees, because there are many and different kinds of them; <u>or are they not rather to be distinguished</u> <u>by some other quality,</u> as for example beauty, size, or shape? How would you answer me?

Men. I should answer that bees do not differ from one another, as bees.

Soc. And if I went on to say: That is what I desire to know, Meno; tell me what is the quality in which they do not differ, but are all alike;-would you be able to answer?

Men. I should.

Soc. And so of the virtues, however many and different they may be, they have all a common nature which makes them virtues; and on this he who would answer the question, "What is virtue?" would do well to have his eye fixed: Do you understand?

Men. I am beginning to understand; but I do not as yet take hold of the question as I could wish.

Soc. When you say, Meno, that there is one virtue of a man, another of a woman, another of a child, and so on, does this apply only to virtue, or would you say the same of health, and size, and strength? Or is the nature of health always the same, whether in man or woman?

Men. I should say that health is the same, both in man and woman.

Soc. And is not this true of size and strength? If a woman is strong, she will be strong by reason of the same form and of the same strength subsisting in her which there is in the man. I mean to say that strength, as strength, whether of man or woman, is the same. Is there any difference?

Men. I think not.

Soc. And will not virtue, as virtue, be the same, whether in a child or in a grown-up person, in a woman or in a man?

Men. I cannot help feeling, Socrates, that this case is different from the others.

[Handwritten margin notes: "Socrates is trying to make Meno define Virtue" and "But Meno doesn't seem to be able to define virtue"]

Soc. But why? Were you not saying that the virtue of a man was to order a state, and the virtue of a woman was to order a house?

Men. I did say so.

Soc. And can either house or state or anything be well ordered without temperance and without justice?

Men. Certainly not.

Soc. Then they who order a state or a house temperately or justly order them with temperance and justice?

Men. Certainly.

Virtue is not neccess- arily linked to your role

Soc. Then both men and women, if they are to be good men and women, must have the same virtues of temperance and justice?

Men. True.

Soc. And can either a young man or an elder one be good, if they are intemperate and unjust?

Men. They cannot.

Soc. They must be <u>temperate and just?</u> */ two cardinal virtues*

Men. Yes.

Soc. Then all men are good in the same way, and by participation in the same virtues?

Men. Such is the inference.

Soc. And they surely would not have been good in the same way, unless their virtue had been the same?

Men. They would not.

Soc. Then now that the sameness of all virtue has been proven, try and remember what you and Gorgias say that virtue is.

Men. Will you have one definition of them all?

Soc. That is what I am seeking.

Men. If you want to have one definition of them all, I know not what to say, but that virtue is the <u>power of governing mankind.</u>

1st definition for virtue

Soc. And does this definition of virtue include all virtue? Is virtue the same in a child and in a slave, Meno? Can the child govern his father, or the slave his master; and would he who governed be any longer a slave?

Men. I think not, Socrates.

Soc. No, indeed; there would be small reason in that. Yet once more, fair friend; according to you, virtue is "the power of governing"; but do you not add "justly and not unjustly"?

Men. Yes, Socrates; I agree there; for justice is virtue.

Soc. Would you say "virtue," Meno, or "a virtue"?

Men. What do you mean?

Soc. I mean as I might say about anything; that a round, for example, is "a figure" and not simply "figure," and I should adopt this mode of speaking, because there are other figures.

Men. Quite right; and that is just what I am saying about virtue-that there are other virtues as well as justice.

Soc. What are they? tell me the names of them, as I would tell you the names of the other figures if you asked me.

Men. Courage and temperance and wisdom and magnanimity are virtues; and there are many others.

generosity (large gifts)

Soc. Yes, Meno; and again we are in the same case: in searching after one virtue we have found many, though not in the same way as before; but we have been unable to find the common virtue which runs through them all.

Men. Why, Socrates, even now I am not able to follow you in the attempt to get at one common notion of virtue as of other things.

Soc. No wonder; but I will try to get nearer if I can, for you know that all things have a common notion. Suppose now that some one asked you the question which I asked before: Meno, he would say, what is figure? And if you answered "roundness," he would reply to you, in my way of speaking, by asking whether you would say that roundness is "figure" or "a figure"; and you would answer "a figure."

Men. Certainly.

Soc. And for this reason-that there are other figures?

Men. Yes.

Soc. And if he proceeded to ask, What other figures are there? you would have told him.

Men. I should.

Soc. And if he similarly asked what colour is, and you answered whiteness, and the questioner rejoined, Would you say that whiteness is colour or a colour? you would reply, A colour, because there are other colours as well.

Men. I should.

Soc. And if he had said, Tell me what they are?-you would have told him of other colours which are colours just as much as whiteness.

Men. Yes.

Soc. And suppose that he were to pursue the matter in my way, he would say: Ever and anon we are landed in particulars, but this is not what I want; tell me then, since you call them by a common name, and say that they are all figures, even when opposed to one another, what is that common nature which you designate as figure-which contains straight as well as round, and is no more one than the other-that would be your mode of speaking?

Men. Yes.

whether something is or is something in a broader something

Soc. And in speaking thus, you do not mean to say that the round is round any more than straight, or the straight any more straight than round?

Men. Certainly not.

Soc. You only assert that the round figure is not more a figure than the straight, or the straight than the round?

Men. Very true.

Soc. To what then do we give the name of figure? Try and answer. Suppose that when a person asked you this question either about figure or colour, you were to reply, Man, I do not understand what you want, or know what you are saying; he would look rather astonished and say: Do you not understand that I am looking for the "simile in multis"? And then he might put the question in another form: Mono, he might say, what is that "simile in multis" which you call figure, and which includes not only round and straight figures, but all? Could you not answer that question, Meno? I wish that you would try; the attempt will be good practice with a view to the answer about virtue.

Men. I would rather that you should answer, Socrates.

Soc. Shall I indulge you?

Men. By all means.

Soc. And then you will tell me about virtue?

Men. I will.

Soc. Then I must do my best, for there is a prize to be won.

Men. Certainly.

Soc. Well, I will try and explain to you what figure is. What do you say to this answer?-Figure is the only thing which always follows colour. Will you be satisfied with it, as I am sure that I should be, if you would let me have a similar definition of virtue?

Men. But, Socrates, it is such a simple answer.

Soc. Why simple?

Men. Because, according to you, figure is that which always follows colour.

(Soc. Granted.)

error in Socrates answer

Men. But if a person were to say that he does not know what colour is, any more than what figure is-what sort of answer would you have given him?

Soc. I should have told him the truth. And if he were a philosopher of the eristic and antagonistic sort, I should say to him: You have my answer, and if I am wrong, your business is to take up the argument and refute me. But if we were friends, and were talking as you and I are now, I should reply in a milder strain and more in the dialectician's vein; that is to say, I should not only speak the truth, but I should make use of premisses which the person interrogated would be willing to admit. And this is the way in which I shall endeavour to approach you. You will acknowledge, will you not, that there is such a thing as an end, or termination, or extremity?-all which words use in the same sense, although I am aware that Prodicus might draw distinctions about them: but still you, I am sure, would speak of a thing as ended or terminated-that is all which I am saying-not anything very difficult.

Men. Yes, I should; and I believe that I understand your meaning.

Soc. And you would speak of a surface and also of a solid, as for example in geometry.

Men. Yes.

Soc. Well then, you are now in a condition to understand my definition of figure. I define figure to be that in which the solid ends; or, more concisely, the limit of solid.

Men. And now, Socrates, what is colour?

Soc. You are outrageous, Meno, in thus plaguing a poor old man to give you an answer, when you will not take the trouble of remembering what is Gorgias' definition of virtue.

Men. When you have told me what I ask, I will tell you, Socrates.

Soc. A man who was blindfolded has only to hear you talking, and he would know that you are a fair creature and have still many lovers.

Men. Why do you think so?

Soc. Why, because you always speak in imperatives: like all beauties when they are in their prime, you are tyrannical; and also, as I suspect, you have found out that I have weakness for the fair, and therefore to humour you I must answer.

Men. Please do.

Soc. Would you like me to answer you after the manner of Gorgias, which is familiar to you?

Men. I should like nothing better.

Soc. Do not he and you and Empedocles say that there are certain effluences of existence?

Men. Certainly.

Soc. And passages into which and through which the effluences pass?

Men. Exactly.

Soc. And some of the effluences fit into the passages, and some of them are too small or too large?

Men. True.

Soc. And there is such a thing as sight?

Men. Yes.

Soc. And now, as Pindar says, "read my meaning" colour

A sarcastic & funny exchange between Socrates & Meno

is an effluence of form, commensurate with sight, and palpable to sense.

Men. That, Socrates, appears to me to be an admirable answer.

Color

Soc. Why, yes, because it happens to be one which you have been in the habit of hearing: and your wit will have discovered, I suspect, that you may explain in the same way the nature of sound and smell, and of many other similar phenomena.

Men. Quite true.

Socrates
is
talking
about
how
Meno
prefers
definitions
that he's
used to,
v/s
another
version

Soc. The answer, Meno, was in the orthodox solemn vein, and therefore was more acceptable to you than the other answer about figure.

Men. Yes.

Soc. And yet, O son of Alexidemus, I cannot help thinking that the other was the better; and I am sure that you would be of the same opinion, if you would only stay and be initiated, and were not compelled, as you said yesterday, to go away before the mysteries.

Men. But I will stay, Socrates, if you will give me many such answers.

Soc. Well then, for my own sake as well as for yours, I will do my very best; but I am afraid that I shall not be able to give you very many as good: and now, in your turn, you are to fulfil your promise, and tell me what virtue is in the universal; and do not make a singular into a plural, as the facetious say of those who break a thing, but deliver virtue to me whole and sound, and not broken into a number of pieces: I have given you the pattern.

Men. Well then, Socrates, virtue, as I take it, is when he, who desires the honourable, is able to provide it for himself; so the poet says, and I say too-

Virtue is the desire of things honourable and the pow-

Another definition of Virtue

er of attaining them.

Soc. And does he who desires the honourable also desire the good?

Men. Certainly.

Soc. Then are there some who desire the evil and others who desire the good? Do not all men, my dear sir, desire good?

Men. I think not.

Soc. There are some who desire evil?

Men. Yes.

Soc. Do you mean that they think the evils which they desire, to be good; or do they know that they are evil and yet desire them?

Men. Both, I think.

Soc. And do you really imagine, Meno, that a man knows evils to be evils and desires them notwithstanding?

Men. Certainly I do.

Soc. And desire is of possession?

Men. Yes, of possession.

Soc. And does he think that the evils will do good to him who possesses them, or does he know that they will do him harm?

Men. There are some who think that the evils will do them good, and others who know that they will do them harm.

Soc. And, in your opinion, do those who think that they will do them good know that they are evils?

Men. Certainly not.

Soc. Is it not obvious that those who are ignorant of their

[handwritten margin note: Socrates moves away from virtue temporarily, to talk of the men who desire good and the men who desire evil... and what Meno thinks about it]

nature do not desire them; but they desire what they suppose to be goods although they are really evils; and if they are mistaken and suppose the evils to be good they really desire goods?

Men. Yes, in that case.

Soc. Well, and do those who, as you say, desire evils, and think that evils are hurtful to the possessor of them, know that they will be hurt by them?

Men. They must know it.

Soc. And must they not suppose that those who are hurt are miserable in proportion to the hurt which is inflicted upon them?

Men. How can it be otherwise?

Soc. But are not the miserable ill-fated?

Men. Yes, indeed.

Soc. And does any one desire to be miserable and ill-fated?

Men. I should say not, Socrates.

Soc. But if there is no one who desires to be miserable, there is no one, Meno, who desires evil; for what is misery but the desire and possession of evil?

Men. That appears to be the truth, Socrates, and I admit that nobody desires evil.

Soc. And yet, were you not saying just now that virtue is the desire and power of attaining good?

Men. Yes, I did say so.

Soc. But if this be affirmed, then the desire of good is common to all, and one man is no better than another in that respect?

Men. True.

Soc. And if one man is not better than another in desiring good, he must be better in the power of attaining it?

Men. Exactly.

Soc. Then, according to your definition, virtue would appear to be the power of attaining good?

Meno has altered his definition of virtue

Men. I entirely approve, Socrates, of the manner in which you now view this matter.

Soc. Then let us see whether what you say is true from another point of view; for very likely you may be right:-You affirm virtue to be the power of attaining goods?

Men. Yes.

Soc. And the goods which mean are such as health and wealth and the possession of gold and silver, and having office and honour in the state-those are what you would call goods?

Meno is talking of worldly goods as being virtue not actual good.

Men. Yes, I should include all those.

Soc. Then, according to Meno, who is the hereditary friend of the great king, virtue is the power of getting silver and gold; and would you add that they must be gained piously, justly, or do you deem this to be of no consequence? And is any mode of acquisition, even if unjust and dishonest, equally to be deemed virtue?

Men. Not virtue, Socrates, but vice.

Soc. Then justice or temperance or holiness, or some other part of virtue, as would appear, must accompany the acquisition, and without them the mere acquisition of good will not be virtue.

Men. Why, how can there be virtue without these?

Soc. And the non-acquisition of gold and silver in a dishonest manner for oneself or another, or in other words the want of them, may be equally virtue?

Men. True.

Soc. Then the acquisition of such goods is no more virtue than the non-acquisition and want of them, but whatever is accompanied by justice or honesty is virtue, and whatever is devoid of justice is vice.

Men. It cannot be otherwise, in my judgment.

Soc. And were we not saying just now that justice, temperance, and the like, were each of them a part of virtue?

Men. Yes.

Soc. And so, Meno, this is the way in which you mock me.

Men. Why do you say that, Socrates?

Meno is contradicting himself

Soc. Why, because I asked you to deliver virtue into my hands whole and unbroken, and I gave you a pattern according to which you were to frame your answer; and you have forgotten already, and tell me that virtue is the power of attaining good justly, or with justice; and justice you acknowledge to be a part of virtue.

Men. Yes.

and Socrates is trying to make

Soc. Then it follows from your own admissions, that virtue is doing what you do with a part of virtue; for justice and the like are said by you to be parts of virtue.

Men. What of that?

Meno understand what it is that he's doing.

Soc. What of that! Why, did not I ask you to tell me the nature of virtue as a whole? And you are very far from telling me this; but declare every action to be virtue which is done with a part of virtue; as though you had told me and I must already know the whole of virtue, and this too when frittered away into little pieces. And, therefore, my dear I fear that I must begin again and repeat the same question: What is virtue? for otherwise, I can only say, that every action done with a part of virtue is virtue; what else is the meaning of saying that every action done with justice is virtue? Ought I not to ask the question over again; for can any one who does not know virtue know a part of virtue?

Men. No; I do not say that he can.

Soc. Do you remember how, in the example of figure, we rejected any answer given in terms which were as yet unexplained or unadmitted?

Men. Yes, Socrates; and we were quite right in doing so.

Soc. But then, my friend, do not suppose that we can explain to any one the nature of virtue as a whole through some unexplained portion of virtue, or anything at all in that fashion; we should only have to ask over again the old question, What is virtue? Am I not right?

Men. I believe that you are.

Soc. Then begin again, and answer me, What, according to you and your friend Gorgias, is the definition of virtue?

Socrates repeats their original question as a way of wiping out old and wrong ideas

Men. O Socrates, I used to be told, before I knew you, that you were always doubting yourself and making others doubt; and now you are casting your spells over me, and I am simply getting bewitched and enchanted, and am at my wits' end. And if I may venture to make a jest upon you, you seem to me both in your appearance and in your power over others to be very like the flat torpedo fish, who torpifies those who come near him and touch him, as you have now torpified me, I think. For my soul and my tongue are really torpid, and I do not know how to answer you; and though I have been delivered of an infinite variety of speeches about virtue before now, and to many persons-and very good ones they were, as I thought-at this moment I cannot even say what virtue is. And I think that you are very wise in not voyaging and going away from home, for if you did in other places as do in Athens, you would be cast into prison as a magician.

Meno complains

Soc. You are a rogue, Meno, and had all but caught me.

Men. What do you mean, Socrates?

Soc. I can tell why you made a simile about me.

Men. Why?

Soc. In order that I might make another simile about you. For I know that all pretty young gentlemen like to have pretty similes made about them-as well they may-but I shall not return the compliment. As to my being a torpedo, if the torpedo is torpid as well as the cause of torpidity in others, then indeed I am a torpedo, but not otherwise; for I perplex others, not because I am clear, but because I am utterly perplexed myself. And now I know not what virtue is, and you seem to be in the same case, although you did once perhaps know before you touched me. However, I have no objection to join with you in the enquiry.

Men. And how will you enquire, Socrates, into that which you do not know? What will you put forth as the subject of enquiry? And if you find what you want, how will you ever know that this is the thing which you did not know?

Soc. I know, Meno, what you mean; but just see what a tiresome dispute you are introducing. You argue that man cannot enquire either about that which he knows, or about that which he does not know; for if he knows, he has no need to enquire; and if not, he cannot; for he does not know the, very subject about which he is to enquire.

Men. Well, Socrates, and is not the argument sound?

Soc. I think not.

Men. Why not?

Soc. I will tell you why: I have heard from certain wise men and women who spoke of things divine that-

Men. What did they say?

Soc. They spoke of a glorious truth, as I conceive.

Men. What was it? and who were they?

Soc. Some of them were priests and priestesses, who

had studied how they might be able to give a reason of their profession: there, have been poets also, who spoke of these things by inspiration, like Pindar, and many others who were inspired. And they say-mark, now, and see whether their words are true-they say that the soul of man is immortal, and at one time has an end, which is termed dying, and at another time is born again, but is never destroyed. And the moral is, that a man ought to live always in perfect holiness. "For in the ninth year Persephone sends the souls of those from whom she has received the penalty of ancient crime back again from beneath into the light of the sun above, and these are they who become noble kings and mighty men and great in wisdom and are called saintly heroes in after ages." The soul, then, as being immortal, and having been born again many times, rand having seen all things that exist, whether in this world or in the world below, has knowledge of them all; and it is no wonder that she should be able to call to remembrance all that she ever knew about virtue, and about everything; for as all nature is akin, and the soul has learned all things; there is no difficulty in her eliciting or as men say learning, out of a single recollection -all the rest, if a man is strenuous and does not faint; for all enquiry and all learning is but recollection. And therefore we ought not to listen to this sophistical argument about the impossibility of enquiry: for it will make us idle; and is sweet only to the sluggard; but the other saying will make us active and inquisitive. In that confiding, I will gladly enquire with you into the nature of virtue.

Men. Yes, Socrates; but what do you mean by saying that we do not learn, and that what we call learning is only a process of recollection? Can you teach me how this is?

Soc. I told you, Meno, just now that you were a rogue, and now you ask whether I can teach you, when I am saying that there is no teaching, but only recollection; and thus you imagine that you will involve me in a contradiction.

Men. Indeed, Socrates, I protest that I had no such intention. I only asked the question from habit; but if you can prove to me that what you say is true, I wish that you would.

Soc. It will be no easy matter, but I will try to please you to the utmost of my power. Suppose that you call one of your numerous attendants, that I may demonstrate on him.

Whose house are they in?

Men. Certainly. Come hither, boy.

Soc. He is Greek, and speaks Greek, does he not?

Men. Yes, indeed; he was born in the house.

Soc. Attend now to the questions which I ask him, and observe whether he learns of me or only remembers.

Men. I will.

Soc. Tell me, boy, do you know that a figure like this is a square?

Boy. I do.

Socrates demonstrates on a slave-boy, showing that even the "simplest" boys can understand his message

Soc. And you know that a square figure has these four lines equal?

Boy. Certainly.

Soc. And these lines which I have drawn through the middle of the square are also equal?

Boy. Yes.

Soc. A square may be of any size?

Boy. Certainly.

Soc. And if one side of the figure be of two feet, and the other side be of two feet, how much will the whole be? Let me explain: if in one direction the space was of two feet, and in other direction of one foot, the whole would be of two feet taken once?

Boy. Yes.

Soc. But since this side is also of two feet, there are twice two feet?

Boy. There are.

Soc. Then the square is of twice two feet?

Boy. Yes.

Soc. And how many are twice two feet? count and tell me.

Boy. Four, Socrates.

Soc. And might there not be another square twice as large as this, and having like this the lines equal?

Boy. Yes.

Soc. And of how many feet will that be?

Boy. Of eight feet.

Soc. And now try and tell me the length of the line which forms the side of that double square: this is two feet-what will that be?

Boy. Clearly, Socrates, it will be double.

Soc. Do you observe, Meno, that I am not teaching the boy anything, but only asking him questions; and now he fancies that he knows how long a line is necessary in order to produce a figure of eight square feet; does he not?

Men. Yes.

Soc. And does he really know?

Men. Certainly not.

Soc. He only guesses that because the square is double, the line is double.

Men. True.

Soc. Observe him while he recalls the steps in regular order. (To the Boy.) Tell me, boy, do you assert that a double space comes from a double line? Remember that I am not speaking of an oblong, but of a figure equal every way, and twice the size of this-that is to say of eight feet; and I want to know whether you still say that a double square comes from double line?

Boy. Yes.

Soc. But does not this line become doubled if we add another such line here?

Boy. Certainly.

Soc. And four such lines will make a space containing eight feet?

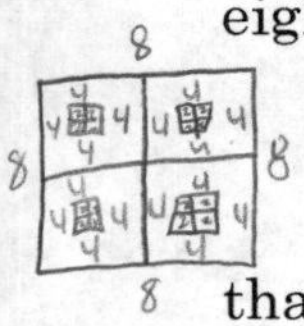

Boy. Yes.

Soc. Let us describe such a figure: Would you not say that this is the figure of eight feet?

Boy. Yes.

Soc. And are there not these four divisions in the figure, each of which is equal to the figure of four feet?

Boy. True.

Soc. And is not that four times four?

Boy. Certainly.

Soc. And four times is not double?

Boy. No, indeed.

Soc. But how much?

Boy. Four times as much.

Soc. Therefore the double line, boy, has given a space, not twice, but four times as much.

Boy. True.

Soc. Four times four are sixteen-are they not?

Boy. Yes.

[handwritten margin note: Socrates is still seeing how much knowledge the slave-boy has gained from knowledge]

Soc. What line would give you a space of right feet, as this gives one of sixteen feet;-do you see?

Boy. Yes.

Soc. And the space of four feet is made from this half line?

Boy. Yes.

Soc. Good; and is not a space of eight feet twice the size of this, and half the size of the other?

Boy. Certainly.

Soc. Such a space, then, will be made out of a line greater than this one, and less than that one?

Boy. Yes; I think so.

Soc. Very good; I like to hear you say what you think. And now tell me, is not this a line of two feet and that of four?

Boy. Yes.

Soc. Then the line which forms the side of eight feet ought to be more than this line of two feet, and less than the other of four feet?

Boy. It ought.

Soc. Try and see if you can tell me how much it will be.

Boy. Three feet.

Soc. Then if we add a half to this line of two, that will be the line of three. Here are two and there is one; and on the other side, here are two also and there is one: and that makes the figure of which you speak?

Boy. Yes.

Soc. But if there are three feet this way and three feet that way, the whole space will be three times three feet?

Boy. That is evident.

Soc. And how much are three times three feet?

Boy. Nine.

Soc. And how much is the double of four?

Boy. Eight.

Soc. Then the figure of eight is not made out of a of three?

Boy. No.

Soc. But from what line?-tell me exactly; and if you would rather not reckon, try and show me the line.

Boy. Indeed, Socrates, I do not know.

Soc. Do you see, Meno, what advances he has made in his power of recollection? He did not know at first, and he does not know now, what is the side of a figure of eight feet: but then he thought that he knew, and answered confidently as if he knew, and had no difficulty; now he has a difficulty, and neither knows nor fancies that he knows.

Men. True.

Soc. Is he not better off in knowing his ignorance?

Men. I think that he is.

Soc. If we have made him doubt, and given him the "torpedo's shock," have we done him any harm?

Men. I think not.

Soc. We have certainly, as would seem, assisted him in some degree to the discovery of the truth; and now he will wish to remedy his ignorance, but then he would have been ready to tell all the world again and again that the double space should have a double side.

Men. True.

Soc. But do you suppose that he would ever have enquired into or learned what he fancied that he knew, though he was really ignorant of it, until he had fallen into perplexity under the idea that he did not know, and had desired to know?

Men. I think not, Socrates.

Soc. Then he was the better for the torpedo's touch?

Men. I think so.

Soc. Mark now the farther development. I shall only ask him, and not teach him, and he shall share the enquiry with me: and do you watch and see if you find me telling or explaining anything to him, instead of eliciting his opinion. Tell me, boy, is not this a square of four feet which I have drawn?

Boy. Yes.

Soc. And now I add another square equal to the former one?

Boy. Yes.

Soc. And a third, which is equal to either of them?

Boy. Yes.

Soc. Suppose that we fill up the vacant corner?

Boy. Very good.

Soc. Here, then, there are four equal spaces?

Boy. Yes.

Soc. And how many times larger is this space than this other?

Boy. Four times.

Soc. But it ought to have been twice only, as you will remember.

Boy. True.

Soc. And does not this line, reaching from corner to corner, bisect each of these spaces?

Boy. Yes.

Soc. And are there not here four equal lines which contain this space?

Boy. There are.

Soc. Look and see how much this space is.

Boy. I do not understand.

Soc. Has not each interior line cut off half of the four spaces?

Boy. Yes.

Soc. And how many spaces are there in this section?

Boy. Four.

Soc. And how many in this?

Boy. Two.

Soc. And four is how many times two?

Boy. Twice.

Soc. And this space is of how many feet?

Boy. Of eight feet.

Soc. And from what line do you get this figure?

Boy. From this.

Soc. That is, from the line which extends from corner to corner of the figure of four feet?

Boy. Yes.

Soc. And that is the line which the learned call the diagonal. And if this is the proper name, then you, Meno's slave,

Socrates
asks the
boy more
about
figures
and now
even I
am
confused

are prepared to affirm that the double space is the square of the diagonal?

Boy. Certainly, Socrates.

Soc. What do you say of him, Meno? Were not all these answers given out of his own head?

Men. Yes, they were all his own.

Soc. And yet, as we were just now saying, he did not know?

Men. True.

Soc. But still he had in him those notions of his-had he not?

Men. Yes.

Soc. Then he who does not know may still have true notions of that which he does not know?

Socrates is now suggesting that one may know something that he doesn't know

Men. He has.

Soc. And at present these notions have just been stirred up in him, as in a dream; but if he were frequently asked the same questions, in different forms, he would know as well as any one at last?

Men. I dare say.

Soc. Without any one teaching him he will recover his knowledge for himself, if he is only asked questions?

Men. Yes.

Soc. And this spontaneous recovery of knowledge in him is recollection?

Men. True.

Soc. And this knowledge which he now has must he not either have acquired or always possessed?

Men. Yes.

Soc. But if he always possessed this knowledge he would always have known; or if he has acquired the knowledge he could not have acquired it in this life, unless he has been taught geometry; for he may be made to do the same with all geometry and every other branch of knowledge. Now, has any one ever taught him all this? You must know about him, if, as you say, he was born and bred in your house.

Men. And I am certain that no one ever did teach him.

Soc. And yet he has the knowledge?

Men. The fact, Socrates, is undeniable.

Soc. But if he did not acquire the knowledge in this life, then he must have had and learned it at some other time?

Men. Clearly he must.

Soc. Which must have been the time when he was not a man?

Men. Yes.

Soc. And if there have been always true thoughts in him, both at the time when he was and was not a man, which only need to be awakened into knowledge by putting questions to him, his soul must have always possessed this knowledge, for he always either was or was not a man?

Men. Obviously.

Soc. And if the truth of all things always existed in the soul, then the soul is immortal. Wherefore be of good cheer, and try to recollect what you do not know, or rather what you do not remember.

Men. I feel, somehow, that I like what you are saying.

Soc. And I, Meno, like what I am saying. Some things I have said of which I am not altogether confident. But that we shall be better and braver and less helpless if we think that we ought to enquire, than we should have been if we indulged in the idle fancy that there was no knowing and no

[handwritten margin notes: The slave is not well-educated / Yet, thanks to Socrates, he has knowledge of geometry and yet, they are only notions that require further explanation]

use in seeking to know what we do not know;-that is a theme upon which I am ready to fight, in word and deed, to the utmost of my power.

Men. There again, Socrates, your words seem to me excellent.

Soc. Then, as we are agreed that a man should enquire about that which he does not know, shall you and I make an effort to enquire together into the nature of virtue?

Men. By all means, Socrates. And yet I would much rather return to my original question, Whether in seeking to acquire virtue we should regard it as a thing to be taught, or as a gift of nature, or as coming to men in some other way?

Soc. Had I the command of you as well as of myself, Meno, I would not have enquired whether virtue is given by instruction or not, until we had first ascertained "what it is." But as you think only of controlling me who am your slave, and never of controlling yourself,-such being your notion of freedom, I must yield to you, for you are irresistible. And therefore I have now to enquire into the qualities of a thing of which I do not as yet know the nature. At any rate, will you condescend a little, and allow the question "Whether virtue is given by instruction, or in any other way," to be argued upon hypothesis? As the geometrician, when he is asked whether a certain triangle is capable being inscribed in a certain circle, will reply: "I cannot tell you as yet; but I will offer a hypothesis which may assist us in forming a conclusion: If the figure be such that when you have produced a given side of it, the given area of the triangle falls short by an area corresponding to the part produced, then one consequence follows, and if this is impossible then some other; and therefore I wish to assume a hypothesis before I tell you whether this triangle is capable of being inscribed in the circle":-that is a geometrical hypothesis. And we too, as we know not the nature and -qualities of virtue, must ask, whether virtue is or not taught, under a hypothesis: as thus, if virtue is of such a class of mental goods, will it be taught or not? Let the first hypothesis be-that virtue is or is not knowledge,-in that case

[handwritten margin note: Meno wishes to ask how to acquire virtue... but Socrates thinks that to answer that correctly, they must ask what virtue is. He must define terms]

[handwritten bottom note: working definition]

will it be taught or not? or, as we were just now saying, re-membered"? For there is no use in disputing about the name. But is virtue taught or not? or rather, does not everyone see that knowledge alone is taught?

Men. I agree.

Soc. Then if virtue is knowledge, virtue will be taught?

Men. Certainly.

Soc. Then now we have made a quick end of this ques-tion: if virtue is of such a nature, it will be taught; and if not, not?

So Meno has come to the conclusion that virtue can both be natural and acquired. Now, they can move on to the next question

Men. Certainly.

Soc. The next question is, whether virtue is knowledge or of another species?

Men. Yes, that appears to be the -question which comes next in order.

Soc. Do we not say that virtue is a good?-This is a hy-pothesis which is not set aside.

Men. Certainly.

Soc. Now, if there be any sort-of good which is distinct from knowledge, virtue may be that good; but if knowledge embraces all good, then we shall be right in think in that virtue is knowledge?

Men. True.

Soc. And virtue makes us good?

Men. Yes.

Soc. And if we are good, then we are profitable; for all good things are profitable?

Men. Yes.

Soc. Then virtue is profitable?

*virtue knowledge ☑
virtue is good ☑*

Men. That is the only inference.

Soc. Then now let us see what are the things which severally profit us. Health and strength, and beauty and wealth—these, and the like of these, we call profitable?

Men. True.

Soc. And yet these things may also sometimes do us harm: would you not think so?

Men. Yes.

Soc. And what is the guiding principle which makes them profitable or the reverse? Are they not profitable when they are rightly used, and hurtful when they are not rightly used?

Men. Certainly.

Soc. Next, let us consider the goods of the soul: they are temperance, justice, courage, quickness of apprehension, memory, magnanimity, and the like?

Men. Surely.

Soc. And such of these as are not knowledge, but of another sort, are sometimes profitable and sometimes hurtful; as, for example, courage wanting prudence, which is only a sort of confidence? When a man has no sense he is harmed by courage, but when he has sense he is profited?

Men. True.

Soc. And the same may be said of temperance and quickness of apprehension; whatever things are learned or done with sense are profitable, but when done without sense they are hurtful?

Men. Very true.

Soc. And in general, all that the attempts or endures, when under the guidance of wisdom, ends in happiness; but when she is under the guidance of folly, in the opposite?

Socrates seems to be slowly leading up to what he thinks that virtue is, and bringing Meno away from his own ideas of virtue

Anything needs to be done with wisdom

Wisdom is therefore more important

Sense is used a lot

Men. That appears to be true.

Soc. If then virtue is a quality of the soul, and is admitted to be profitable, it must be wisdom or prudence, since none of the things of the soul are either profitable or hurtful in themselves, but they are all made profitable or hurtful by the addition of wisdom or of folly; and therefore and therefore if virtue is profitable, virtue must be a sort of wisdom or prudence?

Extremely Close

Men. I quite agree.

Soc. And the other goods, such as wealth and the like, of which we were just now saying that they are sometimes good and sometimes evil, do not they also become profitable or hurtful, accordingly as the soul guides and uses them rightly or wrongly; just as the things of the soul herself are benefited when under the guidance of wisdom and harmed by folly?

Men. True.

Soc. And the wise soul guides them rightly, and the foolish soul wrongly.

Men. Yes.

Socrates is bringing Meno so close to virtue, for now he claims that it's wisdom, one of the Cardinal Virtues

Soc. And is not this universally true of human nature? All other things hang upon the soul, and the things of the soul herself hang upon wisdom, if they are to be good; and so wisdom is inferred to be that which profits-and virtue, as we say, is profitable?

Men. Certainly.

Soc. And thus we arrive at the conclusion that virtue is either wholly or partly wisdom?

Men. I think that what you are saying, Socrates, is very true.

Soc. But if this is true, then the good are not by nature good?

Men. I think not.

Virtue = wisdom (wisdom can't be taught)

Soc. If they had been, there would assuredly have been discerners of characters among us who would have known our future great men; and on their showing we should have adopted them, and when we had got them, we should have kept them in the citadel out of the way of harm, and set a stamp upon them far rather than upon a piece of gold, in order that no one might tamper with them; and when they grew up they would have been useful to the state?

Men. Yes, Socrates, that would have been the right way.

Soc. But if the good are not by nature good, are they made good by instruction?

Men. There appears to be no other alternative, Socrates. On the supposition that virtue is knowledge, there can be no doubt that virtue is taught.

Soc. Yes, indeed; but what if the supposition is erroneous?

Men. I certainly thought just now that we were right.

Soc. Yes, Meno; but a principle which has any soundness should stand firm not only just now, but always.

Men. Well; and why are you so slow of heart to believe that knowledge is virtue?

Soc. I will try and tell you why, Meno. I do not retract the assertion that if virtue is knowledge it may be taught; but I fear that I have some reason in doubting whether virtue is knowledge: for consider now. and say whether virtue, and not only virtue but anything that is taught, must not have teachers and disciples?

Men. Surely.

Soc. And conversely, may not the art of which neither teachers nor disciples exist be assumed to be incapable of being taught?

Men. True; but do you think that there are no teachers

of virtue?

Socrates has never found someone who correctly teaches virtue.

Soc. I have certainly often enquired whether there were any, and taken great pains to find them, and have never succeeded; and many have assisted me in the search, and they were the persons whom I thought the most likely to know. Here at the moment when he is wanted we fortunately have sitting by us Anytus, the very person of whom we should make enquiry; to him then let us repair. In the first Place, he is the son of a wealthy and wise father, Anthemion, who acquired his wealth, not by accident or gift, like Ismenias the Theban (who has recently made himself as rich as Polycrates), but by his own skill and industry, and who is a well-conditioned, modest man, not insolent, or over-bearing, or annoying; moreover, this son of his has received a good education, as the Athenian people certainly appear to think, for they choose him to fill the highest offices. And these are the sort of men from whom you are likely to learn whether there are any teachers of virtue, and who they are. Please, Anytus, to help me and your friend Meno in answering our question, Who are the teachers? Consider the matter thus: If we wanted Meno to be a good physician, to whom should we send him? Should we not send him to the physicians?

Anytus joins our dialogue

Socrates again uses his "questioning strategy" on Anytus to get his opinion out

Any. Certainly.

Soc. Or if we wanted him to be a good cobbler, should we not send him to the cobblers?

Any. Yes.

Soc. And so forth?

Any. Yes.

Soc. Let me trouble you with one more question. When we say that we should be right in sending him to the physicians if we wanted him to be a physician, do we mean that we should be right in sending him to those who profess the art, rather than to those who do not, and to those who demand payment for teaching the art, and profess to teach it to any one who will come and learn? And if these were our reasons, should we not be right in sending him?

Any. Yes.

Soc. And might not the same be said of flute-playing, and of the other arts? Would a man who wanted to make another a flute-player refuse to send him to those who profess to teach the art for money, and be plaguing other persons to give him instruction, who are not professed teachers and who never had a single disciple in that branch of knowledge which he wishes him to acquire-would not such conduct be the height of folly?

Anytus swears by his highest God

Any. Yes, by Zeus, and of ignorance too.

Soc. Very good. And now you are in a position to advise with me about my friend Meno. He has been telling me, Anytus, that he desires to attain that kind of wisdom and-virtue by which men order the state or the house, and honour their parents, and know when to receive and when to send away citizens and strangers, as a good man should. Now, to whom should he go in order that he may learn this virtue? Does not the previous argument imply clearly that we should send him to those who profess and avouch that they are the common teachers of all Hellas, and are ready to impart instruction to any one who likes, at a fixed price?

Socrates seems to have already known of some men who taught wisdom, but he wanted Anytus to answer

Any. Whom do you mean, Socrates?

Soc. You surely know, do you not, Anytus, that these are the people whom mankind call Sophists?

anytus likes to swear by his gods   *← Gorgias is a sophist*

Any. By Heracles, Socrates, forbear! I only hope that no friend or kinsman or acquaintance of mine, whether citizen or stranger, will ever be so mad as to allow himself to be corrupted by them; for they are a manifest pest and corrupting influences to those who have to do with them.

Soc. What, Anytus? Of all the people who profess that they know how to do men good, do you mean to say that these are the only ones who not only do them no good, but positively corrupt those who are entrusted to them, and in return for this disservice have the face to demand money?

Indeed, I cannot believe you; for I know of a single man, (Protagoras) who made more out of his craft than the illustrious Pheidias, who created such noble works, or any ten other statuaries. How could that A mender of old shoes, or patcher up of clothes, who made the shoes or clothes worse than he received them, could not have remained thirty days undetected, and would very soon have starved; whereas during more than forty years, Protagoras was corrupting all Hellas, and sending his disciples from him worse than he received them, and he was never found out. For, if I am not mistaken,-he was about seventy years old at his death, forty of which were spent in the practice of his profession; and during all that time he had a good reputation, which to this day he retains: and not only Protagoras, but many others are well spoken of; some who lived before him, and others who are still living. Now, when you say that they deceived and corrupted the youth, are they to be supposed to have corrupted them consciously or unconsciously? Can those who were deemed by many to be the wisest men of Hellas have been out of their minds?

Socrates is surprised by Anytus' reaction to his suggestion and explains it

Any. Out of their minds! No, Socrates; the young men who gave their money to them, were out of their minds, and their relations and guardians who entrusted their youth to the care of these men were still more out of their minds, and most of all, the cities who allowed them to come in, and did not drive them out, citizen and stranger alike.

Soc. Has any of the Sophists wronged you, Anytus? What makes you so angry with them?

Any. No, indeed, neither I nor any of my belongings has ever had, nor would I suffer them to have, anything to do with them.

Soc. Then you are entirely unacquainted with them?

Any. And I have no wish to be acquainted.

Soc. Then, my dear friend, how can you know whether a thing is good or bad of which you are wholly ignorant?

Any. Quite well; I am sure that I know what manner of men these are, whether I am acquainted with them or not.

Soc. You must be a diviner, Anytus, for I really cannot make out, judging from your own words, how, if you are not acquainted with them, you know about them. But I am not enquiring of you who are the teachers who will corrupt Meno (let them be, if you please, the Sophists); I only ask you to tell him who there is in this great city who will teach him how to become eminent in the virtues which I was just, now describing. He is the friend of your family, and you will oblige him.

Socrates brings the conversation back to his original question of virtue teachers

Any. Why do you not tell him yourself?

Soc. I have told him whom I supposed to be the teachers of these things; but I learn from you that I am utterly at fault, and I dare say that you are right. And now I wish that you, on your part, would tell me to whom among the Athenians he should go. Whom would you name?

Any. Why single out individuals? Any Athenian gentleman, taken at random, if he will mind him, will do far more, good to him than the Sophists.

Soc. And did those gentlemen grow of themselves; and without having been taught by any one, were they nevertheless able to teach others that which they had never learned themselves?

Any. I imagine that they learned of the previous generation of gentlemen. Have there not been many good men in this city?

Anytus thinks that virtue is taught by the past generation

Soc. Yes, certainly, Anytus; and many good statesmen also there always have been and there are still, in the city of Athens. But the question is whether they were also good teachers of their own virtue;-not whether there are, or have been, good men in this part of the world, but whether virtue can be taught, is the question which we have been discussing. Now, do we mean to say that the good men our own and of other times knew how to impart to others that virtue which they had themselves; or is virtue a thing incapable of being communicated or imparted by one man to another? That is the question which I and Meno have been arguing. Look at the matter in your own way: Would you not admit that Themistocles was a good man?

Any. Certainly; no man better.

Soc. And must not he then have been a good teacher, if any man ever was a good teacher, of his own virtue?

Any. Yes certainly,-if he wanted to be so.

Soc. But would he not have wanted? He would, at any rate, have desired to make his own son a good man and a gentleman; he could not have been jealous of him, or have intentionally abstained from imparting to him his own virtue. Did you never hear that he made his son Cleophantus a famous horseman; and had him taught to stand upright on horseback and hurl a javelin, and to do many other marvellous things; and in anything which could be learned from a master he was well trained? Have you not heard from our elders of him?

Any. I have.

Soc. Then no one could say that his son showed any want of capacity?

Any. Very likely not.

Soc. But did any one, old or young, ever say in your hearing that Cleophantus, son of Themistocles, was a wise or good man, as his father was?

Any. I have certainly never heard any one say so.

Soc. And if virtue could have been taught, would his father Themistocles have sought to train him in these minor accomplishments, and allowed him who, as you must remember, was his own son, to be no better than his neighbours in those qualities in which he himself excelled?

Any. Indeed, indeed, I think not.

Soc. Here was a teacher of virtue whom you admit to be among the best men of the past. Let us take another,- Aristides, the son of Lysimachus: would you not acknowledge that he was a good man?

Any. To be sure I should.

Soc. And did not he train his son Lysimachus better than any other Athenian in all that could be done for him by the help of masters? But what has been the result? Is he a bit better than any other mortal? He is an acquaintance of yours, and you see what he is like. There is Pericles, again, magnificent in his wisdom; and he, as you are aware, had two sons, Paralus and Xanthippus.

Any. I know.

Soc. And you know, also, that he taught them to be un- rivalled horsemen, and had them trained in music and gym- nastics and all sorts of arts-in these respects they were on a level with the best-and had he no wish to make good men of them? Nay, he must have wished it. But virtue, as I suspect, could not be taught. And that you may not suppose the incom- petent teachers to be only the meaner sort of Athenians and few in number, remember again that Thucydides had two sons, Melesias and Stephanus, whom, besides giving them a good education in other things, he trained in wrestling, and they were the best wrestlers in Athens: one of them he com- mitted to the care of Xanthias, and the other of Eudorus, who had the reputation of being the most celebrated wrestlers of that day. Do you remember them?

Any. I have heard of them.

Soc. Now, can there be a doubt that Thucydides, whose children were taught things for which he had to spend mon- ey, would have taught them to be good men, which would have cost him nothing, if virtue could have been taught? Will you reply that he was a mean man, and had not many friends among the Athenians and allies? Nay, but he was of a great family, and a man of influence at Athens and in all Hellas, and, if virtue could have been taught, he would have found

[handwritten margin note: Socrates gives more example of good men and how their sons turned out to cement the idea of virtue not being passed down through generation]

[margin: Socrates]
[margin: refuses answer to Meno's question]

out some Athenian or foreigner who would have made good men of his sons, if he could not himself spare the time from cares of state. Once more, I suspect, friend Anytus, that virtue is not a thing which can be taught?

Any. Socrates, I think that you are too ready to speak evil of men: and, if you will take my advice, I would recommend you to be careful. Perhaps there is no city in which it is not easier to do men harm than to do them good, and this is certainly the case at Athens, as I believe that you know.

[margin: false; unjustified injury of a good reputation of another]

Soc. O Meno, think that Anytus is in a rage. And he may well be in a rage, for he thinks, in the first place, that I am defaming these gentlemen; and in the second place, he is of opinion that he is one of them himself. But some day he will know what is the meaning of defamation, and if he ever does, he will forgive me. Meanwhile I will return to you, Meno; for I suppose that there are gentlemen in your region too?

Men. Certainly there are.

[margin: Socrates switches to Thessaly's men, to give Meno a far more personal conclusion to his question but also almost laughing at]

Soc. And are they willing to teach the young? and do they profess to be teachers? and do they agree that virtue is taught?

Men. No indeed, Socrates, they are anything but agreed; you may hear them saying at one time that virtue can be taught, and then again the reverse.

Soc. Can we call those teachers who do not acknowledge the possibility of their own vocation?

Men. I think not, Socrates.

Soc. And what do you think of these Sophists, who are the only professors? Do they seem to you to be teachers of virtue?

Men. I often wonder, Socrates, that Gorgias is never heard promising to teach virtue: and when he hears others promising he only laughs at them; but he thinks that men should be taught to speak.

[margin bottom: the "wise" Thessalonians & Gorgias. So like him. Meno is realizing that Gorgias contradicts himself]

Soc. Then do you not think that the Sophists are teachers?

Men. I cannot tell you, Socrates; like the rest of the world, I am in doubt, and sometimes I think that they are teachers and sometimes not.

Soc. And are you aware that not you only and other politicians have doubts whether virtue can be taught or not, but that Theognis the poet says the very same thing?

Men. Where does he say so?

Soc. In these elegiac verses:

suitable or solemn or distinct

Eat and drink and sit with the mighty, and make yourself agreeable to them; for from the good you will learn what is good, but if you mix with the bad you will lose the intelligence which you already have.

Do you observe that here he seems to imply that virtue can be taught?

Men. Clearly.

Soc. But in some other verses he shifts about and says:

If understanding could be created and put into a man, then they [who were able to perform this feat] would have obtained great rewards.

And again:-

Never would a bad son have sprung from a good sire, for he would have heard the voice of instruction; but not by teaching will you ever make a bad man into a good one.

And this, as you may remark, is a contradiction of the other.

Men. Clearly.

Soc. And is there anything else of which the professors are affirmed not only not to be teachers of others, but to be ignorant themselves, and bad at the knowledge of that which

But Socrates is now bringing in the 中 opposite answer and showing validity which shows how open Socrates is to new ideas

they are professing to teach? or is there anything about which even the acknowledged "gentlemen" are sometimes saying that "this thing can be taught," and sometimes the opposite? Can you say that they are teachers in any true sense whose ideas are in such confusion?

Some teachers contradict themselves

Men. I should say, certainly not.

Soc. But if neither the Sophists nor the gentlemen are teachers, clearly there can be no other teachers?

Men. No.

Soc. And if there are no teachers, neither are there disciples?

Men. Agreed.

They conclude that virtue cannot be taught...

Soc. And we have admitted that a thing cannot be taught of which there are neither teachers nor disciples?

Men. We have.

Soc. And there are no teachers of virtue to be found anywhere?

Men. There are not.

At last! They have an answer!

Soc. And if there are no teachers, neither are there scholars?

Men. That, I think, is true.

Soc. Then virtue cannot be taught?

Men. Not if we are right in our view. But I cannot believe, Socrates, that there are no good men: And if there are, how did they come into existence?

Soc. I am afraid, Meno, that you and I are not good for much, and that Gorgias has been as poor an educator of you as Prodicus has been of me. Certainly we shall have to look to ourselves, and try to find some one who will help in some way or other to improve us. This I say, because I observe that in the previous discussion none of us remarked that right and good action is possible to man under other guidance than that of knowledge (episteme);-and indeed if this be denied, there is no seeing how there can be any good men at all.

Meno wonders if there are any good men

Men. How do you mean, Socrates?

Soc. I mean that good men are necessarily useful or profitable. Were we not right in admitting this? It must be so.

Men. Yes.

Soc. And in supposing that they will be useful only if they are true guides to us of action-there we were also right?

Men. Yes.

Soc. But when we said that a man cannot be a good guide unless he have knowledge (phrhonesis), this we were wrong.

Men. What do you mean by the word "right"?

Soc. I will explain. If a man knew the way to Larisa, or anywhere else, and went to the place and led others thither, would he not be a right and good guide?

After this long back and forth, they conclude that there is not only right action but also right opinion that guides good men in virtue

Men. Certainly.

Soc. And a person who had a right opinion about the way, but had never been and did not know, might be a good guide also, might he not?

Men. Certainly.

Soc. And while he has true opinion about that which the other knows, he will be just as good a guide if he thinks the truth, as he who knows the truth?

Men. Exactly.

Soc. Then true opinion is as good a guide to correct action as knowledge; and that was the point which we omitted in our speculation about the nature of virtue, when we said that knowledge only is the guide of right action; whereas there is also right opinion.

Men. True.

Soc. Then right opinion is not less useful than knowledge?

Men. The difference, Socrates, is only that he who has knowledge will always be right; but he who has right opinion will sometimes be right, and sometimes not.

Soc. What do you mean? Can he be wrong who has right opinion, so long as he has right opinion?

— thoughtfulness ?

Men. I admit the cogency of your argument, and therefore, Socrates, I wonder that knowledge should be preferred to right opinion-or why they should ever differ.

Soc. And shall I explain this wonder to you?

Men. Do tell me.

Socrates claims that

Soc. You would not wonder if you had ever observed the images of Daedalus; but perhaps you have not got them in your country?

Men. What have they to do with the question?

true opinion becomes true knowledge when they are cemented into your mind, but they're not valuable if they leave your soul nice

Soc. Because they require to be fastened in order to keep them, and if they are not fastened they will play truant and run away.

Men. Well. what of that?

Soc. I mean to say that they are not very valuable possessions if they are at liberty, for they will walk off like runaway slaves; but when fastened, they are of great value, for they are really beautiful works of art. Now this is an illustration of the nature of true opinions: while they abide with us they are beautiful and fruitful, but they run away out of the human soul, and do not remain long, and therefore they are not of much value until they are fastened by the tie of the cause; and this fastening of them, friend Meno, is recollection, as you and I have agreed to call it. But when they are bound, in the first place, they have the nature of knowledge; and, in the second place, they are abiding. And this is why knowledge is more honourable and excellent than true opinion, because fastened by a chain.

Men. What you are saying, Socrates, seems to be very like the truth.

Soc. I too speak rather in ignorance; I only conjecture. And yet that knowledge differs from true opinion is no matter of conjecture with me. There are not many things which I profess to know, but this is most certainly one of them. *[margin: Socrates is humble]*

Men. Yes, Socrates; and you are quite right in saying so.

Soc. And am I not also right in saying that true opinion leading the way perfects action quite as well as knowledge?

Men. There again, Socrates, I think you are right.

Soc. Then right opinion is not a whit inferior to knowledge, or less useful in action; nor is the man who has right opinion inferior to him who has knowledge?

Men. True.

Soc. And surely the good man has been acknowledged by us to be useful?

Men. Yes.

Soc. Seeing then that men become good and useful to states, not only because they have knowledge, but because they have right opinion, and that neither knowledge nor right opinion is given to man by nature or acquired by him— (do you imagine either of them to be given by nature? *[margin: Socrates is using knowledge and right opinion to answer whether virtue can be taught]*

Men. Not I.)

Soc. Then if they are not given by nature, neither are the good by nature good?

Men. Certainly not.

Soc. And nature being excluded, then came the question whether virtue is acquired by teaching?

Men. Yes.

Soc. If virtue was wisdom [or knowledge], then, as we thought, it was taught?

Men. Yes.

Soc. And if it was taught it was wisdom?

Men. Certainly.

Soc. And if there were teachers, it might be taught; and if there were no teachers, not?

Men. True.

They'd decided that Virtue is not wisdom, but Socrates has contradicted himself

Soc. But surely we acknowledged that there were no teachers of virtue?

Men. Yes.

Soc. Then we acknowledged that it was not taught, and was not wisdom?

Men. Certainly.

Soc. And yet we admitted that it was a good?

Men. Yes.

Soc. And the right guide is useful and good?

Men. Certainly.

Soc. And the only right guides are knowledge and true opinion-these are the guides of man; for things which happen by chance are not under the guidance of man: but the guides of man are true opinion and knowledge.

Men. I think so too.

Soc. But if virtue is not taught, neither is virtue knowledge.

Men. Clearly not.

Soc. Then of two good and useful things, one, which is

knowledge, has been set aside, and cannot be supposed to be our guide in political life.

Men. I think not.

Soc. And therefore not by any wisdom, and not because they were wise, did Themistocles and those others of whom Anytus spoke govern states. This was the reason why they were unable to make others like themselves-because their virtue was not grounded on knowledge.

Men. That is probably true, Socrates.

Soc. But if not by knowledge, the only alternative which remains is that statesmen must have guided states by right opinion, which is in politics what divination is in religion; for diviners and also prophets say many things truly, but they know not what they say.

Men. So I believe.

Soc. And may we not, Meno, truly call those men "divine" who, having no understanding, yet succeed in many a grand deed and word?

Men. Certainly.

Soc. Then we shall also be right in calling divine those whom we were just now speaking of as diviners and prophets, including the whole tribe of poets. Yes, and statesmen above all may be said to be divine and illumined, being inspired and possessed of God, in which condition they say many grand things, not knowing what they say.

Men. Yes.

Soc. And the women too, Meno, call good men divine-do they not? and the Spartans, when they praise a good man, say "that he is a divine man."

Men. And I think, Socrates, that they are right; although very likely our friend Anytus may take offence at the word.

Soc. I da not care; as for Anytus, there will be another

opportunity of talking with him. To sum up our enquiry-the result seems to be, if we are at all right in our view, that virtue is neither natural nor acquired, but an instinct given by God to the virtuous. Nor is the instinct accompanied by reason, unless there may be supposed to be among statesmen some one who is capable of educating statesmen. And if there be such an one, he may be said to be among the living what Homer says that Tiresias was among the dead, "he alone has understanding; but the rest are flitting shades"; and he and his virtue in like manner will be a reality among shadows.

Men. That is excellent, Socrates.

Soc. Then, Meno, the conclusion is that virtue comes to the virtuous by the gift of God. But we shall never know the certain truth until, before asking how virtue is given, we enquire into the actual nature of virtue. I fear that I must go away, but do you, now that you are persuaded yourself, persuade our friend Anytus. And do not let him be so exasperated; if you can conciliate him, you will have done good service to the Athenian people.

-THE END-

V.

Phaedo

PERSONS OF THE DIALOGUE

PHAEDO, who is the narrator of the dialogue to ECHECRATES of Phlius

SOCRATES

APOLLODORUS

SIMMIAS

CEBES

CRITO

ATTENDANT OF THE PRISON

PHAEDO

SCENE: The Prison of Socrates

PLACE OF THE NARRATION: Phlius

Echecrates. Were you yourself, Phaedo, in the prison with Socrates on the day when he drank the poison?

Phaedo. Yes, Echecrates, I was.

Ech. I wish that you would tell me about his death. What did he say in his last hours? We were informed that he died by taking poison, but no one knew anything more; for no Phliasian.ever goes to Athens now, and a long time has elapsed since any Athenian found his way to Phlius, and therefore we had no clear account.

Phaed. Did you not hear of the proceedings at the trial?

Ech. Yes; someone told us about the trial, and we could not understand why, having been condemned, he was put to death, as appeared, not at the time, but long afterwards. What was the reason of this?

Phaed. An accident, Echecrates. The reason was that the stern of the ship which the Athenians send to Delos happened to have been crowned on the day before he was tried.

Ech. What is this ship?

Phaed. This is the ship in which, as the Athenians say, Theseus went to Crete when he took with him the fourteen youths, and was the saviour of them and of himself. And they were said to have vowed to Apollo at the time, that if they were saved they would make an annual pilgrimage to Delos. Now this custom still continues, and the whole period of the voyage to and from Delos, beginning when the priest of Apollo crowns the stern of the ship, is a holy season, during which the city is not allowed to be polluted by public executions; and often, when the vessel is detained by adverse winds, there may be a very considerable delay. As I was saying, the ship was crowned on the day before the trial, and this was the reason why Socrates lay in prison and was not put to death until long after he was condemned.

Ech. What was the manner of his death, Phaedo? What was said or done? And which of his friends had he with him? Or were they not allowed by the authorities to be present? And did he die alone?

Phaed. No; there were several of his friends with him.

Ech. If you have nothing to do, I wish that you would tell me what passed, as exactly as you can.

Phaed. I have nothing to do, and will try to gratify your wish. For to me, too, there is no greater pleasure than to have Socrates brought to my recollection, whether I speak myself or hear another speak of him.

Ech. You will have listeners who are of the same mind with you, and I hope that you will be as exact as you can.

Phaed. I remember the strange feeling which came over me at being with him. For I could hardly believe that I was present at the death of a friend, and therefore I did not pity him, Echecrates; his mien and his language were so noble and fearless in the hour of death that to me he appeared blessed. I thought that in going to the other world he could not be without a divine call, and that he would be happy, if any man ever was, when he arrived there, and therefore I did not pity him as might seem natural at such a time. But neither could I feel the pleasure which I usually felt in philosophical discourse (for philosophy was the theme of which we spoke). I was pleased, and I was also pained, because I knew that he was soon to die, and this strange mixture of feeling was shared by us all; we were laughing and weeping by turns, especially the excitable Apollodorus-you know the sort of man?

Ech. Yes.

Phaed. He was quite overcome; and I myself and all of us were greatly moved.

Ech. Who were present?

Phaed. Of native Athenians there were, besides Apollodorus, Critobulus and his father Crito, Hermogenes, Epigenes, Aeschines, and Antisthenes; likewise Ctesippus of the deme of Paeania, Menexenus, and some others; but Plato, if I am not mistaken, was ill.

Ech. Were there any strangers?

Phaed. Yes, there were; Simmias the Theban, and Cebes, and Phaedondes; Euclid and Terpison, who came from Megara.

Ech. And was Aristippus there, and Cleombrotus?

Phaed. No, they were said to be in Aegina.

Ech. Anyone else?

Phaed. I think that these were about all.

Ech. And what was the discourse of which you spoke?

Phaed. I will begin at the beginning, and endeavor to repeat the entire conversation. You must understand that we had been previously in the habit of assembling early in the morning at the court in which the trial was held, and which is not far from the prison. There we remained talking with one another until the opening of the prison doors (for they were not opened very early), and then went in and generally passed the day with Socrates. On the last morning the meeting was earlier than usual; this was owing to our having heard on the previous evening that the sacred ship had arrived from Delos, and therefore we agreed to meet very early at the accustomed place. On our going to the prison, the jailer who answered the door, instead of admitting us, came out and bade us wait and he would call us. "For the Eleven," he said, "are now with Socrates; they are taking off his chains, and giving orders that he is to die to-day." He soon returned and said that we might come in. On entering we found Socrates just released from chains, and Xanthippe, whom you know, sitting by him, and holding his child

in her arms. When she saw us she uttered a cry and said, as
women will: "O Socrates, this is the last time that either you
will converse with your friends, or they with you." Socrates
turned to Crito and said: "Crito, let someone take her home."
Some of Crito's people accordingly led her away, crying out
and beating herself. And when she was gone, Socrates, sitting up on the couch, began to bend and rub his leg, saying,
as he rubbed: "How singular is the thing called pleasure, and
how curiously related to pain, which might be thought to be
the opposite of it; for they never come to a man together,
and yet he who pursues either of them is generally compelled
to take the other. They are two, and yet they grow together
out of one head or stem; and I cannot help thinking that if
Aesop had noticed them, he would have made a fable about
God trying to reconcile their strife, and when he could not,
he fastened their heads together; and this is the reason why
when one comes the other follows, as I find in my own case
pleasure comes following after the pain in my leg, which was
caused by the chain."

Upon this Cebes said: I am very glad indeed, Socrates,
that you mentioned the name of Aesop. For that reminds me
of a question which has been asked by others, and was asked
of me only the day before yesterday by Evenus the poet, and
as he will be sure to ask again, you may as well tell me what
I should say to him, if you would like him to have an answer.
He wanted to know why you who never before wrote a line
of poetry, now that you are in prison are putting Aesop into
verse, and also composing that hymn in honor of Apollo.

Tell him, Cebes, he replied, that I had no idea of rivalling
him or his poems; which is the truth, for I knew that I could
not do that. But I wanted to see whether I could purge away
a scruple which I felt about certain dreams. In the course of
my life I have often had intimations in dreams "that I should
make music." The same dream came to me sometimes in one
form, and sometimes in another, but always saying the same
or nearly the same words: Make and cultivate music, said
the dream. And hitherto I had imagined that this was only
intended to exhort and encourage me in the study of philoso-

phy, which has always been the pursuit of my life, and is the noblest and best of music. The dream was bidding me to do what I was already doing, in the same way that the competitor in a race is bidden by the spectators to run when he is already running. But I was not certain of this, as the dream might have meant music in the popular sense of the word, and being under sentence of death, and the festival giving me a respite, I thought that I should be safer if I satisfied the scruple, and, in obedience to the dream, composed a few verses before I departed. And first I made a hymn in honor of the god of the festival, and then considering that a poet, if he is really to be a poet or maker, should not only put words together but make stories, and as I have no invention, I took some fables of esop, which I had ready at hand and knew, and turned them into verse. Tell Evenus this, and bid him be of good cheer; that I would have him come after me if he be a wise man, and not tarry; and that to-day I am likely to be going, for the Athenians say that I must.

Simmias said: What a message for such a man! having been a frequent companion of his, I should say that, as far as I know him, he will never take your advice unless he is obliged.

Why, said Socrates,-is not Evenus a philosopher?

I think that he is, said Simmias.

Then he, or any man who has the spirit of philosophy, will be willing to die, though he will not take his own life, for that is held not to be right.

Here he changed his position, and put his legs off the couch on to the ground, and during the rest of the conversation he remained sitting.

Why do you say, inquired Cebes, that a man ought not to take his own life, but that the philosopher will be ready to follow the dying?

Socrates replied: And have you, Cebes and Simmias, who are acquainted with Philolaus, never heard him speak of this?

I never understood him, Socrates.

My words, too, are only an echo; but I am very willing to say what I have heard: and indeed, as I am going to another place, I ought to be thinking and talking of the nature of the pilgrimage which I am about to make. What can I do better in the interval between this and the setting of the sun?

Then tell me, Socrates, why is suicide held not to be right? as I have certainly heard Philolaus affirm when he was staying with us at Thebes: and there are others who say the same, although none of them has ever made me understand him.

But do your best, replied Socrates, and the day may come when you will understand. I suppose that you wonder why, as most things which are evil may be accidentally good, this is to be the only exception (for may not death, too, be better than life in some cases?), and why, when a man is better dead, he is not permitted to be his own benefactor, but must wait for the hand of another.

By Jupiter! yes, indeed, said Cebes, laughing, and speaking in his native Doric.

I admit the appearance of inconsistency, replied Socrates, but there may not be any real inconsistency after all in this. There is a doctrine uttered in secret that man is a prisoner who has no right to open the door of his prison and run away; this is a great mystery which I do not quite understand. Yet I, too, believe that the gods are our guardians, and that we are a possession of theirs. Do you not agree?

Yes, I agree to that, said Cebes.

And if one of your own possessions, an ox or an ass, for example took the liberty of putting himself out of the way when you had given no intimation of your wish that he should die, would you not be angry with him, and would you not punish him if you could?

Certainly, replied Cebes.

Then there may be reason in saying that a man should wait, and not take his own life until God summons him, as he is now summoning me.

Yes, Socrates, said Cebes, there is surely reason in that. And yet how can you reconcile this seemingly true belief that God is our guardian and we his possessions, with that willingness to die which we were attributing to the philosopher? That the wisest of men should be willing to leave this service in which they are ruled by the gods who are the best of rulers is not reasonable, for surely no wise man thinks that when set at liberty he can take better care of himself than the gods take of him. A fool may perhaps think this-he may argue that he had better run away from his master, not considering that his duty is to remain to the end, and not to run away from the good, and that there is no sense in his running away. But the wise man will want to be ever with him who is better than himself. Now this, Socrates, is the reverse of what was just now said; for upon this view the wise man should sorrow and the fool rejoice at passing out of life.

The earnestness of Cebes seemed to please Socrates. Here, said he, turning to us, is a man who is always inquiring, and is not to be convinced all in a moment, nor by every argument.

And in this case, added Simmias, his objection does appear to me to have some force. For what can be the meaning of a truly wise man wanting to fly away and lightly leave a master who is better than himself? And I rather imagine that Cebes is referring to you; he thinks that you are too ready to leave us, and too ready to leave the gods who, as you acknowledge, are our good rulers.

Yes, replied Socrates; there is reason in that. And this indictment you think that I ought to answer as if I were in court?

That is what we should like, said Simmias.

Then I must try to make a better impression upon you
than I did when defending myself before the judges. For I
am quite ready to acknowledge, Simmias and Cebes, that I
ought to be grieved at death, if I were not persuaded that I
am going to other gods who are wise and good (of this I am as
certain as I can be of anything of the sort) and to men departed (though I am not so certain of this), who are better than
those whom I leave behind; and therefore I do not grieve as I
might have done, for I have good hope that there is yet something remaining for the dead, and, as has been said of old,
some far better thing for the good than for the evil.

But do you mean to take away your thoughts with you,
Socrates? said Simmias. Will you not communicate them to
us?-the benefit is one in which we too may hope to share.
Moreover, if you succeed in convincing us, that will be an
answer to the charge against yourself.

I will do my best, replied Socrates. But you must first
let me hear what Crito wants; he was going to say something
to me.

Only this, Socrates, replied Crito: the attendant who is
to give you the poison has been telling me that you are not to
talk much, and he wants me to let you know this; for that by
talking heat is increased, and this interferes with the action
of the poison; those who excite themselves are sometimes
obliged to drink the poison two or three times.

Then, said Socrates, let him mind his business and be
prepared to give the poison two or three times, if necessary;
that is all.

I was almost certain that you would say that, replied
Crito; but I was obliged to satisfy him.

Never mind him, he said.

And now I will make answer to you, O my judges, and
show that he who has lived as a true philosopher has reason
to be of good cheer when he is about to die, and that after
death he may hope to receive the greatest good in the other

world. And how this may be, Simmias and Cebes, I will endeavor to explain. For I deem that the true disciple of philosophy is likely to be misunderstood by other men; they do not perceive that he is ever pursuing death and dying; and if this is true, why, having had the desire of death all his life long, should he repine at the arrival of that which he has been always pursuing and desiring?

Simmias laughed and said: Though not in a laughing humor, I swear that I cannot help laughing when I think what the wicked world will say when they hear this. They will say that this is very true, and our people at home will agree with them in saying that the life which philosophers desire is truly death, and that they have found them out to be deserving of the death which they desire.

And they are right, Simmias, in saying this, with the exception of the words "They have found them out"; for they have not found out what is the nature of this death which the true philosopher desires, or how he deserves or desires death. But let us leave them and have a word with ourselves: Do we believe that there is such a thing as death?

To be sure, replied Simmias.

And is this anything but the separation of soul and body? And being dead is the attainment of this separation; when the soul exists in herself, and is parted from the body and the body is parted from the soul-that is death?

Exactly: that and nothing else, he replied.

And what do you say of another question, my friend, about which I should like to have your opinion, and the answer to which will probably throw light on our present inquiry: Do you think that the philosopher ought to care about the pleasures-if they are to be called pleasures-of eating and drinking?

Certainly not, answered Simmias.

And what do you say of the pleasures of love-should he care about them?

By no means.

And will he think much of the other ways of indulging the body-for example, the acquisition of costly raiment, or sandals, or other adornments of the body? Instead of caring about them, does he not rather despise anything more than nature needs? What do you say?

I should say the true philosopher would despise them.

Would you not say that he is entirely concerned with the soul and not with the body? He would like, as far as he can, to be quit of the body and turn to the soul.

That is true.

In matters of this sort philosophers, above all other men, may be observed in every sort of way to dissever the soul from the body.

That is true.

Whereas, Simmias, the rest of the world are of opinion that a life which has no bodily pleasures and no part in them is not worth having; but that he who thinks nothing of bodily pleasures is almost as though he were dead.

That is quite true.

What again shall we say of the actual acquirement of knowledge?-is the body, if invited to share in the inquiry, a hinderer or a helper? I mean to say, have sight and hearing any truth in them? Are they not, as the poets are always telling us, inaccurate witnesses? and yet, if even they are inaccurate and indistinct, what is to be said of the other senses?-for you will allow that they are the best of them?

Certainly, he replied.

Then when does the soul attain truth?-for in attempting to consider anything in company with the body she is obviously deceived.

Yes, that is true.

Then must not existence be revealed to her in thought, if at all?

Yes.

And thought is best when the mind is gathered into herself and none of these things trouble her-neither sounds nor sights nor pain nor any pleasure-when she has as little as possible to do with the body, and has no bodily sense or feeling, but is aspiring after being?

That is true.

And in this the philosopher dishonors the body; his soul runs away from the body and desires to be alone and by herself?

That is true.

Well, but there is another thing, Simmias: Is there or is there not an absolute justice?

Assuredly there is.

And an absolute beauty and absolute good?

Of course.

But did you ever behold any of them with your eyes?

Certainly not.

Or did you ever reach them with any other bodily sense? (and I speak not of these alone, but of absolute greatness, and health, and strength, and of the essence or true nature of everything). Has the reality of them ever been perceived by you through the bodily organs? or rather, is not the nearest approach to the knowledge of their several natures made by him who so orders his intellectual vision as to have the most exact conception of the essence of that which he considers?

Certainly.

And he attains to the knowledge of them in their highest purity who goes to each of them with the mind alone, not al-

lowing when in the act of thought the intrusion or introduc-
tion of sight or any other sense in the company of reason, but
with the very light of the mind in her clearness penetrates
into the very fight of truth in each; he has got rid, as far as
he can, of eyes and ears and of the whole body, which he
conceives of only as a disturbing element, hindering the soul
from the acquisition of knowledge when in company with
her-is not this the sort of man who, if ever man did, is likely
to attain the knowledge of existence?

There is admirable truth in that, Socrates, replied Simmias.

And when they consider all this, must not true philosophers make a reflection, of which they will speak to one another in such words as these: We have found, they will say,
a path of speculation which seems to bring us and the argument to the conclusion that while we are in the body, and
while the soul is mingled with this mass of evil, our desire
will not be satisfied, and our desire is of the truth. For the
body is a source of endless trouble to us by reason of the mere
requirement of food; and also is liable to diseases which overtake and impede us in the search after truth: and by filling
us so full of loves, and lusts, and fears, and fancies, and idols,
and every sort of folly, prevents our ever having, as people
say, so much as a thought. For whence come wars, and fightings, and factions? whence but from the body and the lusts
of the body? For wars are occasioned by the love of money,
and money has to be acquired for the sake and in the service
of the body; and in consequence of all these things the time
which ought to be given to philosophy is lost. Moreover, if
there is time and an inclination toward philosophy, yet the
body introduces a turmoil and confusion and fear into the
course of speculation, and hinders us from seeing the truth:
and all experience shows that if we would have pure knowledge of anything we must be quit of the body, and the soul in
herself must behold all things in themselves: then I suppose
that we shall attain that which we desire, and of which we
say that we are lovers, and that is wisdom, not while we live,
but after death, as the argument shows; for if while in com-

pany with the body the soul cannot have pure knowledge, one of two things seems to follow-either knowledge is not to be attained at all, or, if at all, after death. For then, and not till then, the soul will be in herself alone and without the body. In this present life, I reckon that we make the nearest approach to knowledge when we have the least possible concern or interest in the body, and are not saturated with the bodily nature, but remain pure until the hour when God himself is pleased to release us. And then the foolishness of the body will be cleared away and we shall be pure and hold converse with other pure souls, and know of ourselves the clear light everywhere; and this is surely the light of truth. For no impure thing is allowed to approach the pure. These are the sort of words, Simmias, which the true lovers of wisdom cannot help saying to one another, and thinking. You will agree with me in that?

Certainly, Socrates.

But if this is true, O my friend, then there is great hope that, going whither I go, I shall there be satisfied with that which has been the chief concern of you and me in our past lives. And now that the hour of departure is appointed to me, this is the hope with which I depart, and not I only, but every man who believes that he has his mind purified.

Certainly, replied Simmias.

And what is purification but the separation of the soul from the body, as I was saying before; the habit of the soul gathering and collecting herself into herself, out of all the courses of the body; the dwelling in her own place alone, as in another life, so also in this, as far as she can; the release of the soul from the chains of the body?

Very true, he said.

And what is that which is termed death, but this very separation and release of the soul from the body?

To be sure, he said.

And the true philosophers, and they only, study and are

eager to release the soul. Is not the separation and release of the soul from the body their especial study?

That is true.

And as I was saying at first, there would be a ridiculous contradiction in men studying to live as nearly as they can in a state of death, and yet repining when death comes.

Certainly.

Then, Simmias, as the true philosophers are ever studying death, to them, of all men, death is the least terrible. Look at the matter in this way: how inconsistent of them to have been always enemies of the body, and wanting to have the soul alone, and when this is granted to them, to be trembling and repining; instead of rejoicing at their departing to that place where, when they arrive, they hope to gain that which in life they loved (and this was wisdom), and at the same time to be rid of the company of their enemy. Many a man has been willing to go to the world below in the hope of seeing there an earthly love, or wife, or son, and conversing with them. And will he who is a true lover of wisdom, and is persuaded in like manner that only in the world below he can worthily enjoy her, still repine at death? Will he not depart with joy? Surely he will, my friend, if he be a true philosopher. For he will have a firm conviction that there only, and nowhere else, he can find wisdom in her purity. And if this be true, he would be very absurd, as I was saying, if he were to fear death.

He would, indeed, replied Simmias.

And when you see a man who is repining at the approach of death, is not his reluctance a sufficient proof that he is not a lover of wisdom, but a lover of the body, and probably at the same time a lover of either money or power, or both?

That is very true, he replied.

There is a virtue, Simmias, which is named courage. Is not that a special attribute of the philosopher?

Certainly.

Again, there is temperance. Is not the calm, and control, and disdain of the passions which even the many call temperance, a quality belonging only to those who despise the body and live in philosophy?

That is not to be denied.

For the courage and temperance of other men, if you will consider them, are really a contradiction.

How is that, Socrates?

Well, he said, you are aware that death is regarded by men in general as a great evil.

That is true, he said.

And do not courageous men endure death because they are afraid of yet greater evils?

That is true.

Then all but the philosophers are courageous only from fear, and because they are afraid; and yet that a man should be courageous from fear, and because he is a coward, is surely a strange thing.

Very true.

And are not the temperate exactly in the same case? They are temperate because they are intemperate-which may seem to be a contradiction, but is nevertheless the sort of thing which happens with this foolish temperance. For there are pleasures which they must have, and are afraid of losing; and therefore they abstain from one class of pleasures because they are overcome by another: and whereas intemperance is defined as "being under the dominion of pleasure," they overcome only because they are overcome by pleasure. And that is what I mean by saying that they are temperate through intemperance.

That appears to be true.

Yet the exchange of one fear or pleasure or pain for another fear or pleasure or pain, which are measured like coins,
the greater with the less, is not the exchange of virtue. O my
dear Simmias, is there not one true coin for which all things
ought to exchange?-and that is wisdom; and only in exchange
for this, and in company with this, is anything truly bought
or sold, whether courage or temperance or justice. And is
not all true virtue the companion of wisdom, no matter what
fears or pleasures or other similar goods or evils may or may
not attend her? But the virtue which is made up of these
goods, when they are severed from wisdom and exchanged
with one another, is a shadow of virtue only, nor is there any
freedom or health or truth in her; but in the true exchange
there is a purging away of all these things, and temperance,
and justice, and courage, and wisdom herself are a purgation
of them. And I conceive that the founders of the mysteries
had a real meaning and were not mere triflers when they intimated in a figure long ago that he who passes unsanctified
and uninitiated into the world below will live in a slough, but
that he who arrives there after initiation and purification
will dwell with the gods. For "many," as they say in the mysteries, "are the thyrsus bearers, but few are the mystics,"-
meaning, as I interpret the words, the true philosophers. In
the number of whom I have been seeking, according to my
ability, to find a place during my whole life; whether I have
sought in a right way or not, and whether I have succeeded
or not, I shall truly know in a little while, if God will, when I
myself arrive in the other world: that is my belief. And now,
Simmias and Cebes, I have answered those who charge me
with not grieving or repining at parting from you and my
masters in this world; and I am right in not repining, for I
believe that I shall find other masters and friends who are as
good in the world below. But all men cannot believe this, and
I shall be glad if my words have any more success with you
than with the judges of the Athenians.

Cebes answered: I agree, Socrates, in the greater part
of what you say. But in what relates to the soul, men are
apt to be incredulous; they fear that when she leaves the
body her place may be nowhere, and that on the very day of

death she may be destroyed and perish-immediately on her release from the body, issuing forth like smoke or air and vanishing away into nothingness. For if she could only hold together and be herself after she was released from the evils of the body, there would be good reason to hope, Socrates, that what you say is true. But much persuasion and many arguments are required in order to prove that when the man is dead the soul yet exists, and has any force of intelligence.

True, Cebes, said Socrates; and shall I suggest that we talk a little of the probabilities of these things?

I am sure, said Cebes, that I should gready like to know your opinion about them.

I reckon, said Socrates, that no one who heard me now, not even if he were one of my old enemies, the comic poets, could accuse me of idle talking about matters in which I have no concern. Let us, then, if you please, proceed with the inquiry.

Whether the souls of men after death are or are not in the world below, is a question which may be argued in this manner: The ancient doctrine of which I have been speaking affirms that they go from this into the other world, and return hither, and are born from the dead. Now if this be true, and the living come from the dead, then our souls must be in the other world, for if not, how could they be born again? And this would be conclusive, if there were any real evidence that the living are only born from the dead; but if there is no evidence of this, then other arguments will have to be adduced.

That is very true, replied Cebes.

Then let us consider this question, not in relation to man only, but in relation to animals generally, and to plants, and to everything of which there is generation, and the proof will be easier. Are not all things which have opposites generated out of their opposites? I mean such things as good and evil, just and unjust-and there are innumerable other opposites which are generated out of opposites. And I want to show that this holds universally of all opposites; I mean to say, for example, that anything which becomes greater must become greater after being less.

True.

And that which becomes less must have been once greater and then become less.

Yes.

And the weaker is generated from the stronger, and the swifter from the slower.

Very true.

And the worse is from the better, and the more just is from the more unjust.

Of course.

And is this true of all opposites? and are we convinced that all of them are generated out of opposites?

Yes.

And in this universal opposition of all things, are there not also two intermediate processes which are ever going on, from one to the other, and back again; where there is a greater and a less there is also an intermediate process of increase and diminution, and that which grows is said to wax, and that which decays to wane?

Yes, he said.

And there are many other processes, such as division and composition, cooling and heating, which equally involve a passage into and out of one another. And this holds of all opposites, even though not always expressed in words-they are generated out of one another, and there is a passing or process from one to the other of them?

Very true, he replied.

Well, and is there not an opposite of life, as sleep is the opposite of waking?

True, he said.

And what is that?

Death, he answered.

And these, then, are generated, if they are opposites, the one from the other, and have there their two intermediate processes also?

Of course.

Now, said Socrates, I will analyze one of the two pairs of opposites which I have mentioned to you, and also its intermediate processes, and you shall analyze the other to me. The state of sleep is opposed to the state of waking, and out of sleeping waking is generated, and out of waking, sleeping, and the process of generation is in the one case falling asleep, and in the other waking up. Are you agreed about that?

Quite agreed.

Then suppose that you analyze life and death to me in the same manner. Is not death opposed to life?

Yes.

And they are generated one from the other?

Yes.

What is generated from life?

Death.

And what from death?

I can only say in answer-life.

Then the living, whether things or persons, Cebes, are generated from the dead?

That is clear, he replied.

Then the inference is, that our souls are in the world below?

That is true.

And one of the two processes or generations is visible-for surely the act of dying is visible?

Surely, he said.

And may not the other be inferred as the complement of nature, who is not to be supposed to go on one leg only? And if not, a corresponding process of generation in death must also be assigned to her?

Certainly, he replied.

And what is that process?

Revival.

And revival, if there be such a thing, is the birth of the dead into the world of the living?

Quite true.

Then there is a new way in which we arrive at the inference that the living come from the dead, just as the dead come from the living; and if this is true, then the souls of the dead must be in some place out of which they come again. And this, as I think, has been satisfactorily proved.

Yes, Socrates, he said; all this seems to flow necessarily out of our previous admissions.

And that these admissions are not unfair, Cebes, he said, may be shown, as I think, in this way: If generation were in a straight line only, and there were no compensation or circle in nature, no turn or return into one another, then you know that all things would at last have the same form and pass into the same state, and there would be no more generation of them.

What do you mean? he said.

A simple thing enough, which I will illustrate by the case of sleep, he replied. You know that if there were no compensation of sleeping and waking, the story of the sleeping Endymion would in the end have no meaning, because all other things would be asleep, too, and he would not be thought of. Or if there were composition only, and no division of substances, then the chaos of Anaxagoras would come again. And in like manner, my dear Cebes, if all things which partook of life were to die, and after they were dead remained in the form of death, and did not come to life again, all would at last die, and nothing would be alive-how could this be otherwise? For if the living spring from any others who are not the dead, and they die, must not all things at last be swallowed up in death?

There is no escape from that, Socrates, said Cebes; and I think that what you say is entirely true.

Yes, he said, Cebes, I entirely think so, too; and we are not walking in a vain imagination; but I am confident in the belief that there truly is such a thing as living again, and that the living spring from the dead, and that the souls of the dead are in existence, and that the good souls have a better portion than the evil.

Cebes added: Your favorite doctrine, Socrates, that knowledge is simply recollection, if true, also necessarily implies a previous time in which we learned that which we now recollect. But this would be impossible unless our soul was in some place before existing in the human form; here, then, is another argument of the soul's immortality.

But tell me, Cebes, said Simmias, interposing, what proofs are given of this doctrine of recollection? I am not very sure at this moment that I remember them.

One excellent proof, said Cebes, is afforded by questions. If you put a question to a person in a right way, he will give a true answer of himself; but how could he do this unless there were knowledge and right reason already in him? And this is most clearly shown when he is taken to a diagram or to anything of that sort.

But if, said Socrates, you are still incredulous, Simmias, I would ask you whether you may not agree with me when

you look at the matter in another way; I mean, if you are still
incredulous as to whether knowledge is recollection.

Incredulous, I am not, said Simmias; but I want to have
this doctrine of recollection brought to my own recollection,
and, from what Cebes has said, I am beginning to recollect
and be convinced; but I should still like to hear what more
you have to say.

This is what I would say, he replied: We should agree, if
I am not mistaken, that what a man recollects he must have
known at some previous time.

Very true.

And what is the nature of this recollection? And, in asking this, I mean to ask whether, when a person has already
seen or heard or in any way perceived anything, and he
knows not only that, but something else of which he has not
the same, but another knowledge, we may not fairly say that
he recollects that which comes into his mind. Are we agreed
about that?

What do you mean?

I mean what I may illustrate by the following instance:
The knowledge of a lyre is not the same as the knowledge of
a man?

True.

And yet what is the feeling of lovers when they recognize a lyre, or a garment, or anything else which the beloved
has been in the habit of using? Do not they, from knowing
the lyre, form in the mind's eye an image of the youth to
whom the lyre belongs? And this is recollection: and in the
same way anyone who sees Simmias may remember Cebes;
and there are endless other things of the same nature.

Yes, indeed, there are-endless, replied Simmias.

And this sort of thing, he said, is recollection, and is
most commonly a process of recovering that which has been

forgotten through time and inattention.

Very true, he said.

Well; and may you not also from seeing the picture of a horse or a lyre remember a man? and from the picture of Simmias, you may be led to remember Cebes?

True.

Or you may also be led to the recollection of Simmias himself?

True, he said.

And in all these cases, the recollection may be derived from things either like or unlike?

That is true.

And when the recollection is derived from like things, then there is sure to be another question, which is, whether the likeness of that which is recollected is in any way defective or not.

Very true, he said.

And shall we proceed a step further, and affirm that there is such a thing as equality, not of wood with wood, or of stone with stone, but that, over and above this, there is equality in the abstract? Shall we affirm this?

Affirm, yes, and swear to it, replied Simmias, with all the confidence in life.

And do we know the nature of this abstract essence?

To be sure, he said.

And whence did we obtain this knowledge? Did we not see equalities of material things, such as pieces of wood and stones, and gather from them the idea of an equality which is different from them?-you will admit that? Or look at the matter again in this way: Do not the same pieces of wood or stone appear at one time equal, and at another time unequal?

That is certain.

But are real equals ever unequal? or is the idea of equality ever inequality?

That surely was never yet known, Socrates.

Then these (so-called) equals are not the same with the idea of equality?

I should say, clearly not, Socrates.

And yet from these equals, although differing from the idea of equality, you conceived and attained that idea?

Very true, he said.

Which might be like, or might be unlike them?

Yes.

But that makes no difference; whenever from seeing one thing you conceived another, whether like or unlike, there must surely have been an act of recollection?

Very true.

But what would you say of equal portions of wood and stone, or other material equals? and what is the impression produced by them? Are they equals in the same sense as absolute equality? or do they fall short of this in a measure?

Yes, he said, in a very great measure, too.

And must we not allow that when I or anyone look at any object, and perceive that the object aims at being some other thing, but falls short of, and cannot attain to it-he who makes this observation must have had previous knowledge of that to which, as he says, the other, although similar, was inferior?

Certainly.

And has not this been our case in the matter of equals and of absolute equality?

Precisely.

Then we must have known absolute equality previously to the time when we first saw the material equals, and reflected that all these apparent equals aim at this absolute equality, but fall short of it?

That is true.

And we recognize also that this absolute equality has only been known, and can only be known, through the medium of sight or touch, or of some other sense. And this I would affirm of all such conceptions.

Yes, Socrates, as far as the argument is concerned, one of them is the same as the other.

And from the senses, then, is derived the knowledge that all sensible things aim at an idea of equality of which they fall short-is not that true?

Yes.

Then before we began to see or hear or perceive in any way, we must have had a knowledge of absolute equality, or we could not have referred to that the equals which are derived from the senses-for to that they all aspire, and of that they fall short?

That, Socrates, is certainly to be inferred from the previous statements.

And did we not see and hear and acquire our other senses as soon as we were born?

Certainly.

Then we must have acquired the knowledge of the ideal equal at some time previous to this?

Yes.

That is to say, before we were born, I suppose?

True.

And if we acquired this knowledge before we were born, and were born having it, then we also knew before we were born and at the instant of birth not only equal or the greater or the less, but all other ideas; for we are not speaking only of equality absolute, but of beauty, goodness, justice, holiness, and all which we stamp with the name of essence in the dialectical process, when we ask and answer questions. Of all this we may certainly affirm that we acquired the knowledge before birth?

That is true.

But if, after having acquired, we have not forgotten that which we acquired, then we must always have been born with knowledge, and shall always continue to know as long as life lasts-for knowing is the acquiring and retaining knowledge and not forgetting. Is not forgetting, Simmias, just the losing of knowledge?

Quite true, Socrates.

But if the knowledge which we acquired before birth was lost by us at birth, and afterwards by the use of the senses we recovered that which we previously knew, will not that which we call learning be a process of recovering our knowledge, and may not this be rightly termed recollection by us?

Very true.

For this is clear, that when we perceived something, either by the help of sight or hearing, or some other sense, there was no difficulty in receiving from this a conception of some other thing like or unlike which had been forgotten and which was associated with this; and therefore, as I was saying, one of two alternatives follows: either we had this knowledge at birth, and continued to know through life; or, after birth, those who are said to learn only remember, and learning is recollection only.

Yes, that is quite true, Socrates.

And which alternative, Simmias, do you prefer? Had we the knowledge at our birth, or did we remember afterwards the things which we knew previously to our birth?

I cannot decide at the moment.

At any rate you can decide whether he who has knowledge ought or ought not to be able to give a reason for what he knows.

Certainly, he ought.

But do you think that every man is able to give a reason about these very matters of which we are speaking?

I wish that they could, Socrates, but I greatly fear that to-morrow at this time there will be no one able to give a reason worth having.

Then you are not of opinion, Simmias, that all men know these things?

Certainly not.

Then they are in process of recollecting that which they learned before.

Certainly.

But when did our souls acquire this knowledge?-not since we were born as men?

Certainly not.

And therefore previously?

Yes.

Then, Simmias, our souls must have existed before they were in the form of man-without bodies, and must have had intelligence.

Unless indeed you suppose, Socrates, that these notions were given us at the moment of birth; for this is the only time that remains.

Yes, my friend, but when did we lose them? for they are not in us when we are born-that is admitted. Did we lose them at the moment of receiving them, or at some other time?

No, Socrates, I perceive that I was unconsciously talking nonsense.

Then may we not say, Simmias, that if, as we are always repeating, there is an absolute beauty, and goodness, and essence in general, and to this, which is now discovered to be a previous condition of our being, we refer all our sensations, and with this compare them-assuming this to have a prior existence, then our souls must have had a prior existence, but if not, there would be no force in the argument? There can be no doubt that if these absolute ideas existed before we were born, then our souls must have existed before we were born, and if not the ideas, then not the souls.

Yes, Socrates; I am convinced that there is precisely the same necessity for the existence of the soul before birth, and of the essence of which you are speaking: and the argument arrives at a result which happily agrees with my own notion. For there is nothing which to my mind is so evident as that beauty, goodness, and other notions of which you were just now speaking have a most real and absolute existence; and I am satisfied with the proof.

Well, but is Cebes equally satisfied? for I must convince him too.

I think, said Simmias, that Cebes is satisfied: although he is the most incredulous of mortals, yet I believe that he is convinced of the existence of the soul before birth. But that after death the soul will continue to exist is not yet proven even to my own satisfaction. I cannot get rid of the feeling of the many to which Cebes was referring-the feeling that when the man dies the soul may be scattered, and that this may be the end of her. For admitting that she may be generated and created in some other place, and may have existed before entering the human body, why after having entered in and gone out again may she not herself be destroyed and come to an end?

Very true, Simmias, said Cebes; that our soul existed

before we were born was the first half of the argument, and this appears to have been proven; that the soul will exist after death as well as before birth is the other half of which the proof is still wanting, and has to be supplied.

But that proof, Simmias and Cebes, has been already given, said Socrates, if you put the two arguments together-I mean this and the former one, in which we admitted that everything living is born of the dead. For if the soul existed before birth, and in coming to life and being born can be born only from death and dying, must she not after death continue to exist, since she has to be born again? surely the proof which you desire has been already furnished. Still I suspect that you and Simmias would be glad to probe the argument further; like children, you are haunted with a fear that when the soul leaves the body, the wind may really blow her away and scatter her; especially if a man should happen to die in stormy weather and not when the sky is calm.

Cebes answered with a smile: Then, Socrates, you must argue us out of our fears-and yet, strictly speaking, they are not our fears, but there is a child within us to whom death is a sort of hobgoblin; him too we must persuade not to be afraid when he is alone with him in the dark.

Socrates said: Let the voice of the charmer be applied daily until you have charmed him away.

And where shall we find a good charmer of our fears, Socrates, when you are gone?

Hellas, he replied, is a large place, Cebes, and has many good men, and there are barbarous races not a few: seek for him among them all, far and wide, sparing neither pains nor money; for there is no better way of using your money. And you must not forget to seek for him among yourselves too; for he is nowhere more likely to be found.

The search, replied Cebes, shall certainly be made. And now, if you please, let us return to the point of the argument at which we digressed.

By all means, replied Socrates; what else should I please?

Very good, he said.

Must we not, said Socrates, ask ourselves some question of this sort?-What is that which, as we imagine, is liable to be scattered away, and about which we fear? and what again is that about which we have no fear? And then we may proceed to inquire whether that which suffers dispersion is or is not of the nature of soul-our hopes and fears as to our own souls will turn upon that.

That is true, he said.

Now the compound or composite may be supposed to be naturally capable of being dissolved in like manner as of being compounded; but that which is uncompounded, and that only, must be, if anything is, indissoluble.

Yes; that is what I should imagine, said Cebes.

And the uncompounded may be assumed to be the same and unchanging, where the compound is always changing and never the same?

That I also think, he said.

Then now let us return to the previous discussion. Is that idea or essence, which in the dialectical process we define as essence of true existence-whether essence of equality, beauty, or anything else: are these essences, I say, liable at times to some degree of change? or are they each of them always what they are, having the same simple, self-existent and unchanging forms, and not admitting of variation at all, or in any way, or at any time?

They must be always the same, Socrates, replied Cebes.

And what would you say of the many beautiful-whether men or horses or garments or any other things which may be called equal or beautiful-are they all unchanging and the same always, or quite the reverse? May they not rather be described as almost always changing and hardly ever the same either with themselves or with one another?

The latter, replied Cebes; they are always in a state of change.

And these you can touch and see and perceive with the senses, but the unchanging things you can only perceive with the mind-they are invisible and are not seen?

That is very true, he said.

Well, then, he added, let us suppose that there are two sorts of existences, one seen, the other unseen.

Let us suppose them.

The seen is the changing, and the unseen is the unchanging.

That may be also supposed.

And, further, is not one part of us body, and the rest of us soul?

To be sure.

And to which class may we say that the body is more alike and akin?

Clearly to the seen: no one can doubt that.

And is the soul seen or not seen?

Not by man, Socrates.

And by "seen" and "not seen" is meant by us that which is or is not visible to the eye of man?

Yes, to the eye of man.

And what do we say of the soul? is that seen or not seen?

Not seen.

Unseen then?

Yes.

Then the soul is more like to the unseen, and the body to the seen?

That is most certain, Socrates.

And were we not saying long ago that the soul when using the body as an instrument of perception, that is to say, when using the sense of sight or hearing or some other sense (for the meaning of perceiving through the body is perceiving through the senses)-were we not saying that the soul too is then dragged by the body into the region of the changeable, and wanders and is confused; the world spins round her, and she is like a drunkard when under their influence?

Very true.

But when returning into herself she reflects; then she passes into the realm of purity, and eternity, and immortality, and unchangeableness, which are her kindred, and with them she ever lives, when she is by herself and is not let or hindered; then she ceases from her erring ways, and being in communion with the unchanging is unchanging. And this state of the soul is called wisdom?

That is well and truly said, Socrates, he replied.

And to which class is the soul more nearly alike and akin, as far as may be inferred from this argument, as well as from the preceding one?

I think, Socrates, that, in the opinion of everyone who follows the argument, the soul will be infinitely more like the unchangeable even the most stupid person will not deny that.

And the body is more like the changing?

Yes.

Yet once more consider the matter in this light: When

the soul and the body are united, then nature orders the soul
to rule and govern, and the body to obey and serve.

Now which of these two functions is akin to the divine?
and which to the mortal? Does not the divine appear to you
to be that which naturally orders and rules, and the mortal
that which is subject and servant?

True.

And which does the soul resemble?

The soul resembles the divine and the body the mortal-
there can be no doubt of that, Socrates.

Then reflect, Cebes: is not the conclusion of the whole
matter this?-that the soul is in the very likeness of the divine,
and immortal, and intelligible, and uniform, and indissoluble, and unchangeable; and the body is in the very likeness
of the human, and mortal, and unintelligible, and multiform,
and dissoluble, and changeable. Can this, my dear Cebes, be
denied?

No, indeed.

But if this is true, then is not the body liable to speedy
dissolution?

and is not the soul almost or altogether indissoluble?

Certainly.

And do you further observe, that after a man is dead,
the body, which is the visible part of man, and has a visible framework, which is called a corpse, and which would
naturally be dissolved and decomposed and dissipated, is not
dissolved or decomposed at once, but may remain for a good
while, if the constitution be sound at the time of death, and
the season of the year favorable? For the body when shrunk
and embalmed, as is the custom in Egypt, may remain almost entire through infinite ages; and even in decay, still
there are some portions, such as the bones and ligaments,
which are practically indestructible. You allow that?

Yes.

And are we to suppose that the soul, which is invisible, in passing to the true Hades, which like her is invisible, and pure, and noble, and on her way to the good and wise God, whither, if God will, my soul is also soon to go-that the soul, I repeat, if this be her nature and origin, is blown away and perishes immediately on quitting the body as the many say? That can never be, dear Simmias and Cebes. The truth rather is that the soul which is pure at departing draws after her no bodily taint, having never voluntarily had connection with the body, which she is ever avoiding, herself gathered into herself (for such abstraction has been the study of her life). And what does this mean but that she has been a true disciple of philosophy and has practised how to die easily? And is not philosophy the practice of death?

Certainly.

That soul, I say, herself invisible, departs to the invisible worldto the divine and immortal and rational: thither arriving, she lives in bliss and is released from the error and folly of men, their fears and wild passions and all other human ills, and forever dwells, as they say of the initiated, in company with the gods. Is not this true, Cebes?

Yes, said Cebes, beyond a doubt.

But the soul which has been polluted, and is impure at the time of her departure, and is the companion and servant of the body always, and is in love with and fascinated by the body and by the desires and pleasures of the body, until she is led to believe that the truth only exists in a bodily form, which a man may touch and see and taste and use for the purposes of his lusts-the soul, I mean, accustomed to hate and fear and avoid the intellectual principle, which to the bodily eye is dark and invisible, and can be attained only by philosophy-do you suppose that such a soul as this will depart pure and unalloyed?

That is impossible, he replied.

She is engrossed by the corporeal, which the continual association and constant care of the body have made natural to her.

Very true.

And this, my friend, may be conceived to be that heavy, weighty, earthy element of sight by which such a soul is depressed and dragged down again into the visible world, because she is afraid of the invisible and of the world below-prowling about tombs and sepulchres, in the neighborhood of which, as they tell us, are seen certain ghostly apparitions of souls which have not departed pure, but are cloyed with sight and therefore visible.

That is very likely, Socrates.

Yes, that is very likely, Cebes; and these must be the souls, not of the good, but of the evil, who are compelled to wander about such places in payment of the penalty of their former evil way of life; and they continue to wander until the desire which haunts them is satisfied and they are imprisoned in another body. And they may be supposed to be fixed in the same natures which they had in their former life.

What natures do you mean, Socrates?

I mean to say that men who have followed after gluttony, and wantonness, and drunkenness, and have had no thought of avoiding them, would pass into asses and animals of that sort. What do you think?

I think that exceedingly probable.

And those who have chosen the portion of injustice, and tyranny, and violence, will pass into wolves, or into hawks and kites; whither else can we suppose them to go?

Yes, said Cebes; that is doubtless the place of natures such as theirs. And there is no difficulty, he said, in assigning to all of them places answering to their several natures and propensities?

There is not, he said.

Even among them some are happier than others; and the happiest both in themselves and their place of abode are those who have practised the civil and social virtues which are called temperance and justice, and are acquired by habit and attention without philosophy and mind.

Why are they the happiest?

Because they may be expected to pass into some gentle, social nature which is like their own, such as that of bees or ants, or even back again into the form of man, and just and moderate men spring from them.

That is not impossible.

But he who is a philosopher or lover of learning, and is entirely pure at departing, is alone permitted to reach the gods. And this is the reason, Simmias and Cebes, why the true votaries of philosophy abstain from all fleshly lusts, and endure and refuse to give themselves up to them-not because they fear poverty or the ruin of their families, like the lovers of money, and the world in general; nor like the lovers of power and honor, because they dread the dishonor or disgrace of evil deeds.

No, Socrates, that would not become them, said Cebes.

No, indeed, he replied; and therefore they who have a care of their souls, and do not merely live in the fashions of the body, say farewell to all this; they will not walk in the ways of the blind: and when philosophy offers them purification and release from evil, they feel that they ought not to resist her influence, and to her they incline, and whither she leads they follow her.

What do you mean, Socrates?

I will tell you, he said. The lovers of knowledge are conscious that their souls, when philosophy receives them, are simply fastened and glued to their bodies: the soul is only able to view existence through the bars of a prison, and not

in her own nature; she is wallowing in the mire of all ignorance; and philosophy, seeing the terrible nature of her
confinement, and that the captive through desire is led to
conspire in her own captivity (for the lovers of knowledge
are aware that this was the original state of the soul, and
that when she was in this state philosophy received and gently counseled her, and wanted to release her, pointing out to
her that the eye is full of deceit, and also the ear and other
senses, and persuading her to retire from them in all but the
necessary use of them and to be gathered up and collected
into herself, and to trust only to herself and her own intui-
tions of absolute existence, and mistrust that which comes to
her through others and is subject to vicissitude)-philosophy
shows her that this is visible and tangible, but that what
she sees in her own nature is intellectual and invisible. And
the soul of the true philosopher thinks that she ought not
to resist this deliverance, and therefore abstains from pleasures and desires and pains and fears, as far as she is able;
reflecting that when a man has great joys or sorrows or fears
or desires he suffers from them, not the sort of evil which
might be anticipated-as, for example, the loss of his health
or property, which he has sacrificed to his lusts-but he has
suffered an evil greater far, which is the greatest and worst
of all evils, and one of which he never thinks.

And what is that, Socrates? said Cebes.

Why, this: When the feeling of pleasure or pain in the
soul is most intense, all of us naturally suppose that the object of this intense feeling is then plainest and truest: but
this is not the case.

Very true.

And this is the state in which the soul is most enthralled
by the body.

How is that?

Why, because each pleasure and pain is a sort of nail
which nails and rivets the soul to the body, and engrosses
her and makes her believe that to be true which the body af-

firms to be true; and from agreeing with the body and having
the same delights she is obliged to have the same habits and
ways, and is not likely ever to be pure at her departure to the
world below, but is always saturated with the body; so that
she soon sinks into another body and there germinates and
grows, and has therefore no part in the communion of the
divine and pure and simple.

That is most true, Socrates, answered Cebes.

And this, Cebes, is the reason why the true lovers of
knowledge are temperate and brave; and not for the reason
which the world gives.

Certainly not.

Certainly not! For not in that way does the soul of a
philosopher reason; she will not ask philosophy to release
her in order that when released she may deliver herself up
again to the thraldom of pleasures and pains, doing a work
only to be undone again, weaving instead of unweaving her
Penelope's web. But she will make herself a calm of passion
and follow Reason, and dwell in her, beholding the true and
divine (which is not matter of opinion), and thence derive
nourishment. Thus she seeks to live while she lives, and after death she hopes to go to her own kindred and to be freed
from human ills. Never fear, Simmias and Cebes, that a soul
which has been thus nurtured and has had these pursuits,
will at her departure from the body be scattered and blown
away by the winds and be nowhere and nothing.

When Socrates had done speaking, for a considerable
time there was silence; he himself and most of us appeared
to be meditating on what had been said; only Cebes and Simmias spoke a few words to one another. And Socrates observing this asked them what they thought of the argument, and
whether there was anything wanting? For, said he, much is
still open to suspicion and attack, if anyone were disposed to
sift the matter thoroughly. If you are talking of something
else I would rather not interrupt you, but if you are still
doubtful about the argument do not hesitate to say exactly

what you think, and let us have anything better which you can suggest; and if I am likely to be of any use, allow me to help you.

Simmias said: I must confess, Socrates, that doubts did arise in our minds, and each of us was urging and inciting the other to put the question which he wanted to have answered and which neither of us liked to ask, fearing that our importunity might be troublesome under present circumstances.

Socrates smiled and said: O Simmias, how strange that is; I am not very likely to persuade other men that I do not regard my present situation as a misfortune, if I am unable to persuade you, and you will keep fancying that I am at all more troubled now than at any other time. Will you not allow that I have as much of the spirit of prophecy in me as the swans? For they, when they perceive that they must die, having sung all their life long, do then sing more than ever, rejoicing in the thought that they are about to go away to the god whose ministers they are. But men, because they are themselves afraid of death, slanderously affirm of the swans that they sing a lament at the last, not considering that no bird sings when cold, or hungry, or in pain, not even the nightingale, nor the swallow, nor yet the hoopoe; which are said indeed to tune a lay of sorrow, although I do not believe this to be true of them any more than of the swans. But because they are sacred to Apollo and have the gift of prophecy and anticipate the good things of another world, therefore they sing and rejoice in that day more than they ever did before. And I, too, believing myself to be the consecrated servant of the same God, and the fellow servant of the swans, and thinking that I have received from my master gifts of prophecy which are not inferior to theirs, would not go out of life less merrily than the swans. Cease to mind then about this, but speak and ask anything which you like, while the eleven magistrates of Athens allow.

Well, Socrates, said Simmias, then I will tell you my difficulty, and Cebes will tell you his. For I dare say that you, Socrates, feel, as I do, how very hard or almost impossible is the attainment of any certainty about questions such as these in the present life. And yet I should deem him a coward who did not prove what is said about them to the uttermost, or whose heart failed him before he had examined them on every side. For he should persevere until he has attained one of two things: either he should discover or learn the truth about them; or, if this is impossible, I would have him take the best and most irrefragable of human notions, and let this be the raft upon which he sails through life-not without risk, as I admit, if he cannot find some word of God which will more surely and safely carry him. And now, as you bid me, I will venture to question you, as I should not like to reproach myself hereafter with not having said at the time what I think. For when I consider the matter either alone or with Cebes, the argument does certainly appear to me, Socrates, to be not sufficient.

Socrates answered: I dare say, my friend, that you may be right, but I should like to know in what respect the argument is not sufficient.

In this respect, replied Simmias: Might not a person use the same argument about harmony and the lyre-might he not say that harmony is a thing invisible, incorporeal, fair, divine, abiding in the lyre which is harmonized, but that the lyre and the strings are matter and material, composite, earthy, and akin to mortality? And when someone breaks the lyre, or cuts and rends the strings, then he who takes this view would argue as you do, and on the same analogy, that the harmony survives and has not perished; for you cannot imagine, as we would say, that the lyre without the strings, and the broken strings themselves, remain, and yet that the harmony, which is of heavenly and immortal nature and kindred, has perished-and perished too before the mortal. The harmony, he would say, certainly exists somewhere, and the wood and strings will decay before that decays. For I suspect, Socrates, that the notion of the soul which we are all of us inclined to entertain, would also be yours, and that you too would conceive the body to be strung up, and held together, by the elements of hot and cold, wet and dry, and the like, and that the soul is the harmony or due proportionate admixture of them. And, if this is true, the inference clearly is that when the strings of the body are unduly loosened or overstrained through disorder or other injury, then the soul, though most divine, like other harmonies of music or of the works of art, of course perishes at once, although the material remains of the body may last for a considerable time, until they are either decayed or burnt. Now if anyone maintained that the soul, being the harmony of the elements of the body, first perishes in that which is called death, how shall we answer him?

Socrates looked round at us as his manner was, and said, with a smile: Simmias has reason on his side; and why does not some one of you who is abler than myself answer him? for there is force in his attack upon me. But perhaps, before we answer him, we had better also hear what Cebes has to say against the argument-this will give us time for reflection, and when both of them have spoken, we may either assent to them if their words appear to be in consonance with the truth, or if not, we may take up the other side, and argue with them. Please to tell me then, Cebes, he said, what was the difficulty which troubled you?

Cebes said: I will tell you. My feeling is that the argument is still in the same position, and open to the same objections which were urged before; for I am ready to admit that the existence of the soul before entering into the bodily form has been very ingeniously, and, as I may be allowed to say, quite sufficiently proven; but the existence of the soul after death is still, in my judgment, unproven. Now my objection is not the same as that of Simmias; for I am not disposed to deny that the soul is stronger and more lasting than the body, being of opinion that in all such respects the soul very far excels the body. Well, then, says the argument to me, why do you remain unconvinced? When you see that the weaker is still in existence after the man is dead, will you not admit that the more lasting must also survive during the same period of time? Now I, like Simmias, must employ a figure; and I shall ask you to consider whether the figure is to the point. The parallel which I will suppose is that of an old weaver,

who dies, and after his death somebody says: He is not dead,
he must be alive; and he appeals to the coat which he himself wove and wore, and which is still whole and undecayed.
And then he proceeds to ask of someone who is incredulous,
whether a man lasts longer, or the coat which is in use and
wear; and when he is answered that a man lasts far longer,
thinks that he has thus certainly demonstrated the survival
of the man, who is the more lasting, because the less lasting
remains. But that, Simmias, as I would beg you to observe, is
not the truth; everyone sees that he who talks thus is talking
nonsense. For the truth is that this weaver, having worn and
woven many such coats, though he outlived several of them,
was himself outlived by the last; but this is surely very far
from proving that a man is slighter and weaker than a coat.
Now the relation of the body to the soul may be expressed in
a similar figure; for you may say with reason that the soul is
lasting, and the body weak and short-lived in comparison. And
every soul may be said to wear out many bodies, especially in
the course of a long life. For if while the man is alive the body
deliquesces and decays, and yet the soul always weaves her
garment anew and repairs the waste, then of course, when
the soul perishes, she must have on her last garment, and
this only will survive her; but then again when the soul is
dead the body will at last show its native weakness, and soon
pass into decay. And therefore this is an argument on which
I would rather not rely as proving that the soul exists after
death. For suppose that we grant even more than you affirm
as within the range of possibility, and besides acknowledging
that the soul existed before birth admit also that after death
the souls of some are existing still, and will exist, and will
be born and die again and again, and that there is a natural
strength in the soul which will hold out and be born many
times-for all this, we may be still inclined to think that she
will weary in the labors of successive births, and may at last
succumb in one of her deaths and utterly perish; and this
death and dissolution of the body which brings destruction
to the soul may be unknown to any of us, for no one of us can
have had any experience of it: and if this be true, then I say
that he who is confident in death has but a foolish confidence,

unless he is able to prove that the soul is altogether immortal and imperishable. But if he is not able to prove this, he who is about to die will always have reason to fear that when the body is disunited, the soul also may utterly perish.

All of us, as we afterwards remarked to one another, had an unpleasant feeling at hearing them say this. When we had been so firmly convinced before, now to have our faith shaken seemed to introduce a confusion and uncertainty, not only into the previous argument, but into any future one; either we were not good judges, or there were no real grounds of belief.

Ech. There I feel with you-indeed I do, Phaedo, and when you were speaking, I was beginning to ask myself the same question: What argument can I ever trust again? For what could be more convincing than the argument of Socrates, which has now fallen into discredit? That the soul is a harmony is a doctrine which has always had a wonderful attraction for me, and, when mentioned, came back to me at once, as my own original conviction. And now I must begin again and find another argument which will assure me that when the man is dead the soul dies not with him. Tell me, I beg, how did Socrates proceed? Did he appear to share the unpleasant feeling which you mention? or did he receive the interruption calmly and give a sufficient answer? Tell us, as exactly as you can, what passed.

Phaed. Often, Echecrates, as I have admired Socrates, I never admired him more than at that moment. That he should be able to answer was nothing, but what astonished me was, first, the gentle and pleasant and approving manner in which he regarded the words of the young men, and then his quick sense of the wound which had been inflicted by the argument, and his ready application of the healing art. He might be compared to a general rallying his defeated and broken army, urging them to follow him and return to the field of argument.

Ech. How was that?

Phaed. You shall hear, for I was close to him on his right hand, seated on a sort of stool, and he on a couch which was a good deal higher. Now he had a way of playing with my hair, and then he smoothed my head, and pressed the hair upon my neck, and said: To-morrow, Phaedo, I suppose that these fair locks of yours will be severed.

Yes, Socrates, I suppose that they will, I replied.

Not so if you will take my advice.

What shall I do with them? I said.

To-day, he replied, and not to-morrow, if this argument dies and cannot be brought to life again by us, you and I will both shave our locks; and if I were you, and could not maintain my ground against Simmias and Cebes, I would myself take an oath, like the Argives, not to wear hair any more until I had renewed the conflict and defeated them.

Yes, I said, but Heracles himself is said not to be a match for two.

Summon me then, he said, and I will be your Iolaus until the sun goes down.

I summon you rather, I said, not as Heracles summoning Iolaus, but as Iolaus might summon Heracles.

That will be all the same, he said. But first let us take care that we avoid a danger.

And what is that? I said.

The danger of becoming misologists, he replied, which is one of the very worst things that can happen to us. For as there are misanthropists or haters of men, there are also misologists or haters of ideas, and both spring from the same cause, which is ignorance of the world. Misanthropy arises from the too great confidence of inexperience; you trust a man and think him altogether true and good and faithful, and then in a little while he turns out to be false and knavish; and then another and another, and when this has hap-

pened several times to a man, especially within the circle of
his most trusted friends, as he deems them, and he has often
quarreled with them, he at last hates all men, and believes
that no one has any good in him at all. I dare say that you
must have observed this.

Yes, I said.

And is not this discreditable? The reason is that a man,
having to deal with other men, has no knowledge of them; for
if he had knowledge he would have known the true state of
the case, that few are the good and few the evil, and that the
great majority are in the interval between them.

How do you mean? I said.

I mean, he replied, as you might say of the very large
and very small, that nothing is more uncommon than a very
large or a very small man; and this applies generally to all
extremes, whether of great and small, or swift and slow, or
fair and foul, or black and white: and whether the instances
you select be men or dogs or anything else, few are the extremes, but many are in the mean between them. Did you
never observe this?

Yes, I said, I have.

And do you not imagine, he said, that if there were a
competition of evil, the first in evil would be found to be very
few?

Yes, that is very likely, I said.

Yes, that is very likely, he replied; not that in this respect arguments are like men-there I was led on by you to
say more than I had intended; but the point of comparison
was that when a simple man who has no skill in dialectics believes an argument to be true which he afterwards imagines
to be false, whether really false or not, and then another and
another, he has no longer any faith left, and great disputers,
as you know, come to think, at last that they have grown to
be the wisest of mankind; for they alone perceive the utter
unsoundness and instability of all arguments, or, indeed, of

all things, which, like the currents in the Euripus, are going
up and down in never-ceasing ebb and flow.

That is quite true, I said.

Yes, Phaedo, he replied, and very melancholy too, if
there be such a thing as truth or certainty or power of knowing at all, that a man should have lighted upon some argument or other which at first seemed true and then turned
out to be false, and instead of blaming himself and his own
want of wit, because he is annoyed, should at last be too glad
to transfer the blame from himself to arguments in general;
and forever afterwards should hate and revile them, and lose
the truth and knowledge of existence.

Yes, indeed, I said; that is very melancholy.

Let us, then, in the first place, he said, be careful of
admitting into our souls the notion that there is no truth
or health or soundness in any arguments at all; but let us
rather say that there is as yet no health in us, and that we
must quit ourselves like men and do our best to gain health-
you and all other men with a view to the whole of your future
life, and I myself with a view to death. For at this moment
I am sensible that I have not the temper of a philosopher;
like the vulgar, I am only a partisan. For the partisan, when
he is engaged in a dispute, cares nothing about the rights of
the question, but is anxious only to convince his hearers of
his own assertions. And the difference between him and me
at the present moment is only this-that whereas he seeks to
convince his hearers that what he says is true, I am rather
seeking to convince myself; to convince my hearers is a sec-
ondary matter with me. And do but see how much I gain by
this. For if what I say is true, then I do well to be persuaded
of the truth, but if there be nothing after death, still, during
the short time that remains, I shall save my friends from
lamentations, and my ignorance will not last, and therefore
no harm will be done. This is the state of mind, Simmias and
Cebes, in which I approach the argument. And I would ask
you to be thinking of the truth and not of Socrates: agree
with me, if I seem to you to be speaking the truth; or if not,

withstand me might and main, that I may not deceive you as well as myself in my enthusiasm, and, like the bee, leave my sting in you before I die.

And now let us proceed, he said. And first of all let me be sure that I have in my mind what you were saying. Simmias, if I remember rightly, has fears and misgivings whether the soul, being in the form of harmony, although a fairer and diviner thing than the body, may not perish first. On the other hand, Cebes appeared to grant that the soul was more lasting than the body, but he said that no one could know whether the soul, after having worn out many bodies, might not perish herself and leave her last body behind her; and that this is death, which is the destruction not of the body but of the soul, for in the body the work of destruction is ever going on. Are not these, Simmias and Cebes, the points which we have to consider?

They both agreed to this statement of them.

He proceeded: And did you deny the force of the whole preceding argument, or of a part only?

Of a part only, they replied.

And what did you think, he said, of that part of the argument in which we said that knowledge was recollection only, and inferred from this that the soul must have previously existed somewhere else before she was enclosed in the body? Cebes said that he had been wonderfully impressed by that part of the argument, and that his conviction remained unshaken. Simmias agreed, and added that he himself could hardly imagine the possibility of his ever thinking differently about that.

But, rejoined Socrates, you will have to think differently, my Theban friend, if you still maintain that harmony is a compound, and that the soul is a harmony which is made out of strings set in the frame of the body; for you will surely never allow yourself to say that a harmony is prior to the elements which compose the harmony.

No, Socrates, that is impossible.

But do you not see that you are saying this when you say that the soul existed before she took the form and body of man, and was made up of elements which as yet had no existence? For harmony is not a sort of thing like the soul, as you suppose; but first the lyre, and the strings, and the sounds exist in a state of discord, and then harmony is made last of all, and perishes first. And how can such a notion of the soul as this agree with the other?

Not at all, replied Simmias.

And yet, he said, there surely ought to be harmony when harmony is the theme of discourse.

There ought, replied Simmias.

But there is no harmony, he said, in the two propositions that knowledge is recollection, and that the soul is a harmony. Which of them, then, will you retain?

I think, he replied, that I have a much stronger faith, Socrates, in the first of the two, which has been fully demonstrated to me, than in the latter, which has not been demonstrated at all, but rests only on probable and plausible grounds; and I know too well that these arguments from probabilities are impostors, and unless great caution is observed in the use of them they are apt to be deceptive-in geometry, and in other things too. But the doctrine of knowledge and recollection has been proven to me on trustworthy grounds; and the proof was that the soul must have existed before she came into the body, because to her belongs the essence of which the very name implies existence. Having, as I am convinced, rightly accepted this conclusion, and on sufficient grounds, I must, as I suppose, cease to argue or allow others to argue that the soul is a harmony.

Let me put the matter, Simmias, he said, in another point of view: Do you imagine that a harmony or any other composition can be in a state other than that of the elements out of which it is compounded?

Certainly not.

Or do or suffer anything other than they do or suffer?

He agreed.

Then a harmony does not lead the parts or elements which make up the harmony, but only follows them.

He assented.

For harmony cannot possibly have any motion, or sound, or other quality which is opposed to the parts.

That would be impossible, he replied.

And does not every harmony depend upon the manner in which the elements are harmonized?

I do not understand you, he said.

I mean to say that a harmony admits of degrees, and is more of a harmony, and more completely a harmony, when more completely harmonized, if that be possible; and less of a harmony, and less completely a harmony, when less harmonized.

True.

But does the soul admit of degrees? or is one soul in the very least degree more or less, or more or less completely, a soul than another?

Not in the least.

Yet surely one soul is said to have intelligence and virtue, and to be good, and another soul is said to have folly and vice, and to be an evil soul: and this is said truly?

Yes, truly.

But what will those who maintain the soul to be a harmony say of this presence of virtue and vice in the soul?-Will they say that there is another harmony, and another discord, and that the virtuous soul is harmonized, and herself being a harmony has another harmony within her, and that the vicious soul is inharmonical and has no harmony within her?

I cannot say, replied Simmias; but I suppose that something of that kind would be asserted by those who take this view.

And the admission is already made that no soul is more a soul than another; and this is equivalent to admitting that harmony is not more or less harmony, or more or less completely a harmony?

Quite true.

And that which is not more or less a harmony is not more or less harmonized?

True.

And that which is not more or less harmonized cannot have more or less of harmony, but only an equal harmony?

Yes, an equal harmony.

Then one soul not being more or less absolutely a soul than another, is not more or less harmonized?

Exactly.

And therefore has neither more nor less of harmony or of discord?

She has not.

And having neither more nor less of harmony or of discord, one soul has no more vice or virtue than another, if vice be discord and virtue harmony?

Not at all more.

Or speaking more correctly, Simmias, the soul, if she is a harmony, will never have any vice; because a harmony, being absolutely a harmony, has no part in the inharmonical?

No.

And therefore a soul which is absolutely a soul has no vice?

How can she have, consistently with the preceding argument?

Then, according to this, if the souls of all animals are equally and absolutely souls, they will be equally good?

I agree with you, Socrates, he said.

And can all this be true, think you? he said; and are all these consequences admissible-which nevertheless seem to follow from the assumption that the soul is a harmony?

Certainly not, he said.

Once more, he said, what ruling principle is there of human things other than the soul, and especially the wise soul? Do you know of any?

Indeed, I do not.

And is the soul in agreement with the affections of the body? or is she at variance with them? For example, when the body is hot and thirsty, does not the soul incline us against drinking? and when the body is hungry, against eating? And this is only one instance out of ten thousand of the opposition of the soul to the things of the body.

Very true.

But we have already acknowledged that the soul, being a harmony, can never utter a note at variance with the tensions and relaxations and vibrations and other affections of the strings out of which she is composed; she can only follow, she cannot lead them?

Yes, he said, we acknowledged that, certainly.

And yet do we not now discover the soul to be doing the exact opposite-leading the elements of which she is believed to be composed; almost always opposing and coercing them in all sorts of ways throughout life, sometimes more violently with the pains of medicine and gymnastic; then again more gently; threatening and also reprimanding the desires, passions, fears, as if talking to a thing which is not herself, as Homer in the "Odyssey" represents Odysseus doing in the words,

"He beat his breast, and thus reproached his heart:

Endure, my heart; far worse hast thou endured!"

Do you think that Homer could have written this under the idea that the soul is a harmony capable of being led by the affections of the body, and not rather of a nature which leads and masters them; and herself a far diviner thing than any harmony?

Yes, Socrates, I quite agree to that.

Then, my friend, we can never be right in saying that the soul is a harmony, for that would clearly contradict the divine Homer as well as ourselves.

True, he said.

Thus much, said Socrates, of Harmonia, your Theban goddess, Cebes, who has not been ungracious to us, I think; but what shall I say to the Theban Cadmus, and how shall I propitiate him?

I think that you will discover a way of propitiating him, said Cebes; I am sure that you have answered the argument about harmony in a manner that I could never have expected. For when Simmias mentioned his objection, I quite imagined that no answer could be given to him, and therefore I was surprised at finding that his argument could not sustain the first onset of yours; and not impossibly the other, whom you call Cadmus, may share a similar fate.

Nay, my good friend, said Socrates, let us not boast, lest some evil eye should put to flight the word which I am about to speak. That, however, may be left in the hands of those above, while I draw near in Homeric fashion, and try the mettle of your words. Briefly, the sum of your objection is as follows: You want to have proven to you that the soul is imperishable and immortal, and you think that the philosopher who is confident in death has but a vain and foolish confidence, if he thinks that he will fare better than one who has led another sort of life, in the world below, unless he can prove this; and you say that the demonstration of the strength and divinity of the soul, and of her existence prior to our becoming men, does not necessarily imply her immortality. Granting that the soul is longlived, and has known and done much in a former state, still she is not on that account immortal; and her entrance into the human form may be a sort of disease which is the beginning of dissolution, and may at last, after the toils of life are over, end in that which is called death. And whether the soul enters into the body once only or many times, that, as you would say, makes no difference in the fears of individuals. For any man, who is not devoid of natural feeling, has reason to fear, if he has no knowledge or proof of the soul's immortality. That is what I suppose you to say, Cebes, which I designedly repeat, in order that nothing may escape us, and that you may, if you wish, add or subtract anything.

But, said Cebes, as far as I can see at present, I have nothing to add or subtract; you have expressed my meaning.

Socrates paused awhile, and seemed to be absorbed in reflection. At length he said: This is a very serious inquiry which you are raising, Cebes, involving the whole question of generation and corruption, about which I will, if you like, give you my own experience; and you can apply this, if you think that anything which I say will avail towards the solution of your difficulty.

I should very much like, said Cebes, to hear what you have to say.

Then I will tell you, said Socrates. When I was young, Cebes, I had a prodigious desire to know that department of philosophy which is called Natural Science; this appeared to me to have lofty aims, as being the science which has to do

with the causes of things, and which teaches why a thing is,
and is created and destroyed; and I was always agitating myself with the consideration of such questions as these: Is the
growth of animals the result of some decay which the hot and
cold principle contracts, as some have said? Is the blood the
element with which we think, or the air, or the fire? or perhaps nothing of this sort-but the brain may be the originating
power of the perceptions of hearing and sight and smell, and
memory and opinion may come from them, and science may
be based on memory and opinion when no longer in motion,
but at rest. And then I went on to examine the decay of them,
and then to the things of heaven and earth, and at last I
concluded that I was wholly incapable of these inquiries, as I
will satisfactorily prove to you. For I was fascinated by them
to such a degree that my eyes grew blind to things that I had
seemed to myself, and also to others, to know quite well; and
I forgot what I had before thought to be self-evident, that
the growth of man is the result of eating and drinking; for
when by the digestion of food flesh is added to flesh and bone
to bone, and whenever there is an aggregation of congenial
elements, the lesser bulk becomes larger and the small man
greater. Was not that a reasonable notion?

Yes, said Cebes, I think so.

Well; but let me tell you something more. There was a
time when I thought that I understood the meaning of greater and less pretty well; and when I saw a great man standing
by a little one I fancied that one was taller than the other by
a head; or one horse would appear to be greater than another
horse: and still more clearly did I seem to perceive that ten is
two more than eight, and that two cubits are more than one,
because two is twice one.

And what is now your notion of such matters? said
Cebes.

I should be far enough from imagining, he replied, that
I knew the cause of any of them, indeed I should, for I cannot satisfy myself that when one is added to one, the one
to which the addition is made becomes two, or that the two

units added together make two by reason of the addition. For I cannot understand how, when separated from the other, each of them was one and not two, and now, when they are brought together, the mere juxtaposition of them can be the cause of their becoming two: nor can I understand how the division of one is the way to make two; for then a different cause would produce the same effect-as in the former instance the addition and juxtaposition of one to one was the cause of two, in this the separation and subtraction of one from the other would be the cause. Nor am I any longer satisfied that I understand the reason why one or anything else either is generated or destroyed or is at all, but I have in my mind some confused notion of another method, and can never admit this.

Then I heard someone who had a book of Anaxagoras, as he said, out of which he read that mind was the disposer and cause of all, and I was quite delighted at the notion of this, which appeared admirable, and I said to myself: If mind is the disposer, mind will dispose all for the best, and put each particular in the best place; and I argued that if anyone desired to find out the cause of the generation or destruction or existence of anything, he must find out what state of being or suffering or doing was best for that thing, and therefore a man had only to consider the best for himself and others, and then he would also know the worse, for that the same science comprised both. And I rejoiced to think that I had found in Anaxagoras a teacher of the causes of existence such as I desired, and I imagined that he would tell me first whether the earth is flat or round; and then he would further explain the cause and the necessity of this, and would teach me the nature of the best and show that this was best; and if he said that the earth was in the centre, he would explain that this position was the best, and I should be satisfied if this were shown to me, and not want any other sort of cause. And I thought that I would then go and ask him about the sun and moon and stars, and that he would explain to me their comparative swiftness, and their returnings and various states, and how their several affections, active and passive, were all for the best. For I could not imagine that when he spoke

of mind as the disposer of them, he would give any other account of their being as they are, except that this was best;
and I thought when he had explained to me in detail the
cause of each and the cause of all, he would go on to explain
to me what was best for each and what was best for all. I had
hopes which I would not have sold for much, and I seized the
books and read them as fast as I could in my eagerness to
know the better and the worse.

What hopes I had formed, and how grievously was I disappointed! As I proceeded, I found my philosopher altogether
forsaking mind or any other principle of order, but having recourse to air, and ether, and water, and other eccentricities.
I might compare him to a person who began by maintaining
generally that mind is the cause of the actions of Socrates,
but who, when he endeavored to explain the causes of my
several actions in detail, went on to show that I sit here because my body is made up of bones and muscles; and the
bones, as he would say, are hard and have ligaments which
divide them, and the muscles are elastic, and they cover the
bones, which have also a covering or environment of flesh
and skin which contains them; and as the bones are lifted at
their joints by the contraction or relaxation of the muscles, I
am able to bend my limbs, and this is why I am sitting here
in a curved posture: that is what he would say, and he would
have a similar explanation of my talking to you, which he
would attribute to sound, and air, and hearing, and he would
assign ten thousand other causes of the same sort, forgetting
to mention the true cause, which is that the Athenians have
thought fit to condemn me, and accordingly I have thought
it better and more right to remain here and undergo my sentence; for I am inclined to think that these muscles and bones
of mine would have gone off to Megara or Boeotia-by the dog
of Egypt they would, if they had been guided only by their
own idea of what was best, and if I had not chosen as the better and nobler part, instead of playing truant and running
away, to undergo any punishment which the State inflicts.
There is surely a strange confusion of causes and conditions
in all this. It may be said, indeed, that without bones and
muscles and the other parts of the body I cannot execute my

purposes. But to say that I do as I do because of them, and that this is the way in which mind acts, and not from the choice of the best, is a very careless and idle mode of speaking. I wonder that they cannot distinguish the cause from the condition, which the many, feeling about in the dark, are always mistaking and misnaming. And thus one man makes a vortex all round and steadies the earth by the heaven; another gives the air as a support to the earth, which is a sort of broad trough. Any power which in disposing them as they are disposes them for the best never enters into their minds, nor do they imagine that there is any superhuman strength in that; they rather expect to find another Atlas of the world who is stronger and more everlasting and more containing than the good is, and are clearly of opinion that the obligatory and containing power of the good is as nothing; and yet this is the principle which I would fain learn if anyone would teach me. But as I have failed either to discover myself or to learn of anyone else, the nature of the best, I will exhibit to you, if you like, what I have found to be the second best mode of inquiring into the cause.

I should very much like to hear that, he replied.

Socrates proceeded: I thought that as I had failed in the contemplation of true existence, I ought to be careful that I did not lose the eye of my soul; as people may injure their bodily eye by observing and gazing on the sun during an eclipse, unless they take the precaution of only looking at the image reflected in the water, or in some similar medium. That occurred to me, and I was afraid that my soul might be blinded altogether if I looked at things with my eyes or tried by the help of the senses to apprehend them. And I thought that I had better have recourse to ideas, and seek in them the truth of existence. I dare say that the simile is not perfect-for I am very far from admitting that he who contemplates existence through the medium of ideas, sees them only "through a glass darkly," any more than he who sees them in their working and effects. However, this was the method which I adopted: I first assumed some principle which I judged to be the strongest, and then I affirmed as true whatever seemed to agree with this, whether relating to the cause or to anything else; and that which disagreed I regarded as untrue. But I should like to explain my meaning clearly, as I do not think that you understand me.

No, indeed, replied Cebes, not very well.

There is nothing new, he said, in what I am about to tell you; but only what I have been always and everywhere repeating in the previous discussion and on other occasions: I want to show you the nature of that cause which has occupied my thoughts, and I shall have to go back to those familiar words which are in the mouth of everyone, and first of all assume that there is an absolute beauty and goodness and greatness, and the like; grant me this, and I hope to be able to show you the nature of the cause, and to prove the immortality of the soul.

Cebes said: You may proceed at once with the proof, as I readily grant you this.

Well, he said, then I should like to know whether you agree with me in the next step; for I cannot help thinking that if there be anything beautiful other than absolute beauty, that can only be beautiful in as far as it partakes of absolute beauty-and this I should say of everything. Do you agree in this notion of the cause?

Yes, he said, I agree.

He proceeded: I know nothing and can understand nothing of any other of those wise causes which are alleged; and if a person says to me that the bloom of color, or form, or anything else of that sort is a source of beauty, I leave all that, which is only confusing to me, and simply and singly, and perhaps foolishly, hold and am assured in my own mind that nothing makes a thing beautiful but the presence and participation of beauty in whatever way or manner obtained; for as to the manner I am uncertain, but I stoutly contend that by beauty all beautiful things become beautiful. That appears to me to be the only safe answer that I can give, either to myself or to any other, and to that I cling, in the persuasion that I shall never be overthrown, and that I may safely answer to myself or any other that by beauty beautiful things become beautiful. Do you not agree to that?

Yes, I agree.

And that by greatness only great things become great and greater greater, and by smallness the less becomes less.

True.

Then if a person remarks that A is taller by a head than B, and B less by a head than A, you would refuse to admit this, and would stoutly contend that what you mean is only that the greater is greater by, and by reason of, greatness, and the less is less only by, or by reason of, smallness; and thus you would avoid the danger of saying that the greater is greater and the less by the measure of the head, which is the same in both, and would also avoid the monstrous absurdity of supposing that the greater man is greater by reason of the head, which is small. Would you not be afraid of that?

Indeed, I should, said Cebes, laughing.

In like manner you would be afraid to say that ten exceeded eight by, and by reason of, two; but would say by, and by reason of, number; or that two cubits exceed one cubit not by a half, but by magnitude?-that is what you would say, for there is the same danger in both cases.

Very true, he said.

Again, would you not be cautious of affirming that the addition of one to one, or the division of one, is the cause of two? And you would loudly asseverate that you know of no way in which anything comes into existence except by participation in its own proper essence, and consequently, as far as you know, the only cause of two is the participation in duality; that is the way to make two, and the participation in one is the way to make one. You would say: I will let alone puzzles of division and addition-wiser heads than mine may answer them; inexperienced as I am, and ready to start, as the proverb says, at my own shadow, I cannot afford to give

up the sure ground of a principle. And if anyone assails you
there, you would not mind him, or answer him until you had
seen whether the consequences which follow agree with one
another or not, and when you are further required to give
an explanation of this principle, you would go on to assume
a higher principle, and the best of the higher ones, until you
found a resting-place; but you would not refuse the principle
and the consequences in your reasoning like the Eristics-at
least if you wanted to discover real existence. Not that this
confusion signifies to them who never care or think about the
matter at all, for they have the wit to be well pleased with
themselves, however great may be the turmoil of their ideas.
But you, if you are a philosopher, will, I believe, do as I say.

What you say is most true, said Simmias and Cebes,
both speaking at once.

Ech. Yes, Phaedo; and I don't wonder at their assenting.
Anyone who has the least sense will acknowledge the wonderful clear. of Socrates' reasoning.

Phaed. Certainly, Echecrates; and that was the feeling
of the whole company at the time.

Ech. Yes, and equally of ourselves, who were not of the
company, and are now listening to your recital. But what
followed?

Phaedo. After all this was admitted, and they had agreed
about the existence of ideas and the participation in them of
the other things which derive their names from them, Socrates, if I remember rightly, said:-

This is your way of speaking; and yet when you say that
Simmias is greater than Socrates and less than Phaedo, do
you not predicate of Simmias both greatness and smallness?

Yes, I do.

But still you allow that Simmias does not really exceed
Socrates, as the words may seem to imply, because he is Simmias, but by reason of the size which he has; just as Simmias
does not exceed Socrates because he is Simmias, any more

than because Socrates is Socrates, but because he has smallness when compared with the greatness of Simmias?

True.

And if Phaedo exceeds him in size, that is not because
Phaedo is Phaedo, but because Phaedo has greatness rela-
tively to Simmias, who is comparatively smaller?

That is true.

And therefore Simmias is said to be great, and is also
said to be small, because he is in a mean between them, ex-
ceeding the smallness of the one by his greatness, and allowing the greatness of the other to exceed his smallness. He
added, laughing, I am speaking like a book, but I believe that
what I am now saying is true.

Simmias assented to this.

The reason why I say this is that I want you to agree
with me in thinking, not only that absolute greatness will
never be great and also small, but that greatness in us or
in the concrete will never admit the small or admit of being exceeded: instead of this, one of two things will happen-
either the greater will fly or retire before the opposite, which
is the less, or at the advance of the less will cease to exist;
but will not, if allowing or admitting smallness, be changed
by that; even as I, having received and admitted smallness
when compared with Simmias, remain just as I was, and am
the same small person. And as the idea of greatness cannot
condescend ever to be or become small, in like manner the
smallness in us cannot be or become great; nor can any other
opposite which remains the same ever be or become its own
opposite, but either passes away or perishes in the change.

That, replied Cebes, is quite my notion.

One of the company, though I do not exactly remember
which of them, on hearing this, said: By Heaven, is not this
the direct contrary of what was admitted before-that out of
the greater came the less and out of the less the greater, and
that opposites are simply generated from opposites; whereas

now this seems to be utterly denied.

Socrates inclined his head to the speaker and listened. I like your courage, he said, in reminding us of this. But you do not observe that there is a difference in the two cases. For then we were speaking of opposites in the concrete, and now of the essential opposite which, as is affirmed, neither in us nor in nature can ever be at variance with itself: then, my friend, we were speaking of things in which opposites are inherent and which are called after them, but now about the opposites which are inherent in them and which give their name to them; these essential opposites will never, as we maintain, admit of generation into or out of one another. At the same time, turning to Cebes, he said: Were you at all disconcerted, Cebes, at our friend's objection?

That was not my feeling, said Cebes; and yet I cannot deny that I am apt to be disconcerted.

Then we are agreed after all, said Socrates, that the opposite will never in any case be opposed to itself?

To that we are quite agreed, he replied.

Yet once more let me ask you to consider the question from another point of view, and see whether you agree with me: There is a thing which you term heat, and another thing which you term cold?

Certainly.

But are they the same as fire and snow?

Most assuredly not.

Heat is not the same as fire, nor is cold the same as snow?

No.

And yet you will surely admit that when snow, as before said, is under the influence of heat, they will not remain snow and heat; but at the advance of the heat the snow will either retire or perish?

Very true, he replied.

And the fire too at the advance of the cold will either retire or perish; and when the fire is under the influence of the
cold, they will not remain, as before, fire and cold.

That is true, he said.

And in some cases the name of the idea is not confined to
the idea; but anything else which, not being the idea, exists
only in the form of the idea, may also lay claim to it. I will
try to make this clearer by an example: The odd number is
always called by the name of odd?

Very true.

But is this the only thing which is called odd? Are there
not other things which have their own name, and yet are
called odd, because, although not the same as oddness, they
are never without oddness?-that is what I mean to ask-
whether numbers such as the number three are not of the
class of odd. And there are many other examples: would you
not say, for example, that three may be called by its proper
name, and also be called odd, which is not the same with
three? and this may be said not only of three but also of five,
and every alternate number-each of them without being oddness is odd, and in the same way two and four, and the whole
series of alternate numbers, has every number even, without
being evenness. Do you admit that?

Yes, he said, how can I deny that?

Then now mark the point at which I am aiming: not only
do essential opposites exclude one another, but also concrete
things, which, although not in themselves opposed, contain
opposites; these, I say, also reject the idea which is opposed
to that which is contained in them, and at the advance of that
they either perish or withdraw. There is the number three
for example; will not that endure annihilation or anything
sooner than be converted into an even number, remaining
three?

Very true, said Cebes.

And yet, he said, the number two is certainly not opposed to the number three?

It is not.

Then not only do opposite ideas repel the advance of one another, but also there are other things which repel the approach of opposites.

That is quite true, he said.

Suppose, he said, that we endeavor, if possible, to determine what these are.

By all means.

Are they not, Cebes, such as compel the things of which they have possession, not only to take their own form, but also the form of some opposite?

What do you mean?

I mean, as I was just now saying, and have no need to repeat to you, that those things which are possessed by the number three must not only be three in number, but must also be odd.

Quite true.

And on this oddness, of which the number three has the impress, the opposite idea will never intrude?

No.

And this impress was given by the odd principle?

Yes.

And to the odd is opposed the even?

True.

Then the idea of the even number will never arrive at three?

No.

Then three has no part in the even?

None.

Then the triad or number three is uneven?

Very true.

To return then to my distinction of natures which are not opposites, and yet do not admit opposites: as, in this instance, three, although not opposed to the even, does not any the more admit of the even, but always brings the opposite into play on the other side; or as two does not receive the odd, or fire the cold-from these examples (and there are many more of them) perhaps you may be able to arrive at the general conclusion that not only opposites will not receive opposites, but also that nothing which brings the opposite will admit the opposite of that which it brings in that to which it is brought. And here let me recapitulate-for there is no harm in repetition. The number five will not admit the nature of the even, any more than ten, which is the double of five, will admit the nature of the odd-the double, though not strictly opposed to the odd, rejects the odd altogether. Nor again will parts in the ratio of 3:2, nor any fraction in which there is a half, nor again in which there is a third, admit the notion of the whole, although they are not opposed to the whole. You will agree to that?

Yes, he said, I entirely agree and go along with you in that.

And now, he said, I think that I may begin again; and to the question which I am about to ask I will beg you to give not the old safe answer, but another, of which I will offer you an example; and I hope that you will find in what has been just said another foundation which is as safe. I mean that if anyone asks you "what that is, the inherence of which makes the body hot," you will reply not heat (this is what I call the safe and stupid answer), but fire, a far better answer, which we are now in a condition to give. Or if anyone asks you "why a body is diseased," you will not say from disease, but from fever; and instead of saying that oddness is the cause of odd numbers, you will say that the monad is the cause of them: and so of things in general, as I dare say that you will understand sufficiently without my adducing any further examples.

Yes, he said, I quite understand you.

Tell me, then, what is that the inherence of which will render the body alive?

The soul, he replied.

And is this always the case?

Yes, he said, of course.

Then whatever the soul possesses, to that she comes bearing life?

Yes, certainly.

And is there any opposite to life?

There is, he said.

And what is that?

Death.

Then the soul, as has been acknowledged, will never receive the opposite of what she brings. And now, he said, what did we call that principle which repels the even?

The odd.

And that principle which repels the musical, or the just?

The unmusical, he said, and the unjust.

And what do we call the principle which does not admit of death?

The immortal, he said.

And does the soul admit of death?

No.

Then the soul is immortal?

Yes, he said.

And may we say that this is proven?

Yes, abundantly proven, Socrates, he replied.

And supposing that the odd were imperishable, must not three be imperishable?

Of course.

And if that which is cold were imperishable, when the warm principle came attacking the snow, must not the snow have retired whole and unmelted-for it could never have perished, nor could it have remained and admitted the heat?

True, he said.

Again, if the uncooling or warm principle were imperishable, the fire when assailed by cold would not have perished or have been extinguished, but would have gone away unaffected?

Certainly, he said.

And the same may be said of the immortal: if the immortal is also imperishable, the soul when attacked by death cannot perish; for the preceding argument shows that the soul will not admit of death, or ever be dead, any more than three or the odd number will admit of the even, or fire or the heat in the fire, of the cold. Yet a person may say: "But although the odd will not become even at the approach of the even, why may not the odd perish and the even take the place of the odd?" Now to him who makes this objection, we cannot answer that the odd principle is imperishable; for this has not been acknowledged, but if this had been acknowledged, there would have been no difficulty in contending that at the approach of the even the odd principle and the number three took up their departure; and the same argument would have held good of fire and heat and any other thing.

Very true.

And the same may be said of the immortal: if the immortal is also imperishable, then the soul will be imperishable as well as immortal; but if not, some other proof of her imperishableness will have to be given.

No other proof is needed, he said; for if the immortal, being eternal, is liable to perish, then nothing is imperishable.

Yes, replied Socrates, all men will agree that God, and the essential form of life, and the immortal in general, will never perish.

Yes, all men, he said-that is true; and what is more, gods, if I am not mistaken, as well as men.

Seeing then that the immortal is indestructible, must not the soul, if she is immortal, be also imperishable?

Most certainly.

Then when death attacks a man, the mortal portion of him may be supposed to die, but the immortal goes out of the way of death and is preserved safe and sound?

True.

Then, Cebes, beyond question the soul is immortal and imperishable, and our souls will truly exist in another world!

I am convinced, Socrates, said Cebes, and have nothing more to object; but if my friend Simmias, or anyone else, has any further objection, he had better speak out, and not keep silence, since I do not know how there can ever be a more fitting time to which he can defer the discussion, if there is anything which he wants to say or have said.

But I have nothing more to say, replied Simmias; nor do I see any room for uncertainty, except that which arises necessarily out of the greatness of the subject and the feebleness of man, and which I cannot help feeling.

Yes, Simmias, replied Socrates, that is well said: and more than that, first principles, even if they appear certain, should be carefully considered; and when they are satisfactorily ascertained, then, with a sort of hesitating confidence in human reason, you may, I think, follow the course of the argument; and if this is clear, there will be no need for any further inquiry.

That, he said, is true.

But then, O my friends, he said, if the soul is really immortal, what care should be taken of her, not only in respect of the portion of time which is called life, but of eternity! And the danger of neglecting her from this point of view does indeed appear to be awful. If death had only been the end of all, the wicked would have had a good bargain in dying, for they would have been happily quit not only of their body, but of their own evil together with their souls. But now, as the soul plainly appears to be immortal, there is no release or salvation from evil except the attainment of the highest virtue and wisdom. For the soul when on her progress to the world below takes nothing with her but nurture and education; which are indeed said greatly to benefit or greatly to injure the departed, at the very beginning of its pilgrimage in the other world.

For after death, as they say, the genius of each individual, to whom he belonged in life, leads him to a certain place in which the dead are gathered together for judgment, whence they go into the world below, following the guide who is appointed to conduct them from this world to the other: and when they have there received their due and remained their time, another guide brings them back again after many revolutions of ages. Now this journey to the other world is not, as Aeschylus says in the "Telephus," a single and straight path—no guide would be wanted for that, and no one could miss a single path; but there are many partings of the road, and windings, as I must infer from the rites and sacrifices which are offered to the gods below in places where three ways meet on earth. The wise and orderly soul is conscious of her situation and follows in the path; but the soul which desires

the body, and which, as I was relating before, has long been
fluttering about the lifeless frame and the world of sight, is
after many struggles and many sufferings hardly and with
violence carried away by her attendant genius, and when she
arrives at the place where the other souls are gathered, if she
be impure and have done impure deeds, or been concerned in
foul murders or other crimes which are the brothers of these,
and the works of brothers in crime-from that soul everyone
flees and turns away; no one will be her companion, no one
her guide, but alone she wanders in extremity of evil until
certain times are fulfilled, and when they are fulfilled, she is
borne irresistibly to her own fitting habitation; as every pure
and just soul which has passed through life in the company
and under the guidance of the gods has also her own proper
home.

Now the earth has divers wonderful regions, and is indeed in nature and extent very unlike the notions of geog-
raphers, as I believe on the authority of one who shall be
nameless.

What do you mean, Socrates? said Simmias. I have
myself heard many descriptions of the earth, but I do not
know in what you are putting your faith, and I should like
to know.

Well, Simmias, replied Socrates, the recital of a tale does
not, I think, require the art of Glaucus; and I know not that
the art of Glaucus could prove the truth of my tale, which I
myself should never be able to prove, and even if I could, I
fear, Simmias, that my life would come to an end before the
argument was completed. I may describe to you, however,
the form and regions of the earth according to my conception
of them.

That, said Simmias, will be enough.

Well, then, he said, my conviction is that the earth is a
round body in the center of the heavens, and therefore has
no need of air or any similar force as a support, but is kept
there and hindered from falling or inclining any way by the

equability of the surrounding heaven and by her own equipoise. For that which, being in equipoise, is in the center of
that which is equably diffused, will not incline any way in
any degree, but will always remain in the same state and not
deviate. And this is my first notion.

Which is surely a correct one, said Simmias.

Also I believe that the earth is very vast, and that we
who dwell in the region extending from the river Phasis to
the Pillars of Heracles, along the borders of the sea, are just
like ants or frogs about a marsh, and inhabit a small portion
only, and that many others dwell in many like places. For I
should say that in all parts of the earth there are hollows of
various forms and sizes, into which the water and the mist
and the air collect; and that the true earth is pure and in the
pure heaven, in which also are the stars-that is the heaven
which is commonly spoken of as the ether, of which this is
but the sediment collecting in the hollows of the earth. But
we who live in these hollows are deceived into the notion that
we are dwelling above on the surface of the earth; which is
just as if a creature who was at the bottom of the sea were to
fancy that he was on the surface of the water, and that the
sea was the heaven through which he saw the sun and the
other stars-he having never come to the surface by reason of
his feebleness and sluggishness, and having never lifted up
his head and seen, nor ever heard from one who had seen,
this region which is so much purer and fairer than his own.
Now this is exactly our case: for we are dwelling in a hollow
of the earth, and fancy that we are on the surface; and the
air we call the heaven, and in this we imagine that the stars
move. But this is also owing to our feebleness and sluggishness, which prevent our reaching the surface of the air: for if
any man could arrive at the exterior limit, or take the wings
of a bird and fly upward, like a fish who puts his head out
and sees this world, he would see a world beyond; and, if the
nature of man could sustain the sight, he would acknowledge
that this was the place of the true heaven and the true light
and the true stars. For this earth, and the stones, and the
entire region which surrounds us, are spoilt and corroded,

like the things in the sea which are corroded by the brine; for in the sea too there is hardly any noble or perfect growth, but clefts only, and sand, and an endless slough of mud: and even the shore is not to be compared to the fairer sights of this world. And greater far is the superiority of the other. Now of that upper earth which is under the heaven, I can tell you a charming tale, Simmias, which is well worth hearing.

And we, Socrates, replied Simmias, shall be charmed to listen.

The tale, my friend, he said, is as follows: In the first place, the earth, when looked at from above, is like one of those balls which have leather coverings in twelve pieces, and is of divers colors, of which the colors which painters use on earth are only a sample. But there the whole earth is made up of them, and they are brighter far and clearer than ours; there is a purple of wonderful luster, also the radiance of gold, and the white which is in the earth is whiter than any chalk or snow. Of these and other colors the earth is made up, and they are more in number and fairer than the eye of man has ever seen; and the very hollows (of which I was speaking) filled with air and water are seen like light flashing amid the other colors, and have a color of their own, which gives a sort of unity to the variety of earth. And in this fair region everything that grows-trees, and flowers, and fruits-is in a like degree fairer than any here; and there are hills, and stones in them in a like degree smoother, and more transparent, and fairer in color than our highly valued emeralds and sardonyxes and jaspers, and other gems, which are but minute fragments of them: for there all the stones are like our precious stones, and fairer still. The reason of this is that they are pure, and not, like our precious stones, infected or corroded by the corrupt briny elements which coagulate among us, and which breed foulness and disease both in earth and stones, as well as in animals and plants. They are the jewels of the upper earth, which also shines with gold and silver and the like, and they are visible to sight and large and abundant and found in every region of the earth, and blessed is he who sees them. And upon the earth are animals and men, some in a middle region, others dwelling about the air as we dwell about the sea; others in islands which the air flows round, near the continent: and in a word, the air is used by them as the water and the sea are by us, and the ether is to them what the air is to us. Moreover, the temperament of their seasons is such that they have no disease, and live much longer than we do, and have sight and hearing and smell, and all the other senses, in far greater perfection, in the same degree that air is purer than water or the ether than air. Also they have temples and sacred places in which the gods really dwell, and they hear their voices and receive their answers, and are conscious of them and hold converse with them, and they see the sun, moon, and stars as they really are, and their other blessedness is of a piece with this.

Such is the nature of the whole earth, and of the things which are around the earth; and there are divers regions in the hollows on the face of the globe everywhere, some of them deeper and also wider than that which we inhabit, others deeper and with a narrower opening than ours, and some are shallower and wider; all have numerous perforations, and passages broad and narrow in the interior of the earth, connecting them with one another; and there flows into and out of them, as into basins, a vast tide of water, and huge subterranean streams of perennial rivers, and springs hot and cold, and a great fire, and great rivers of fire, and streams of liquid mud, thin or thick (like the rivers of mud in Sicily, and the lava-streams which follow them), and the regions about which they happen to flow are filled up with them. And there is a sort of swing in the interior of the earth which moves all this up and down. Now the swing is in this wise: There is a chasm which is the vastest of them all, and pierces right through the whole earth; this is that which Homer describes in the words,

"Far off, where is the inmost depth beneath the earth";

and which he in other places, and many other poets, have called Tartarus. And the swing is caused by the streams flowing into and out of this chasm, and they each have the nature of the soil through which they flow. And the reason why the streams are always flowing in and out is that the watery element has no bed or bottom, and is surging and swinging up and down, and the surrounding wind and air do the same; they follow the water up and down, hither and thither, over the earth-just as in respiring the air is always in process of inhalation and exhalation; and the wind swinging with the water in and out produces fearful and irresistible blasts: when the waters retire with a rush into the lower parts of the earth, as they are called, they flow through the earth into those regions, and fill them up as with the alternate motion of a pump, and then when they leave those regions and rush back hither, they again fill the hollows here, and when these are filled, flow through subterranean channels and find their way to their several places, forming seas, and lakes, and rivers, and springs. Thence they again enter the earth, some of them making a long circuit into many lands, others going to few places and those not distant, and again fall into Tartarus, some at a point a good deal lower than that at which they rose, and others not much lower, but all in some degree lower than the point of issue. And some burst forth again on the opposite side, and some on the same side, and some wind round the earth with one or many folds, like the coils of a serpent, and descend as far as they can, but always return and fall into the lake. The rivers on either side can descend only to the center and no further, for to the rivers on both sides the opposite side is a precipice.

Now these rivers are many, and mighty, and diverse, and there are four principal ones, of which the greatest and outermost is that called Oceanus, which flows round the earth in a circle; and in the opposite direction flows Acheron, which passes under the earth through desert places, into the Acherusian Lake: this is the lake to the shores of which the souls of the many go when they are dead, and after waiting an appointed time, which is to some a longer and to some a shorter time, they are sent back again to be born as animals. The third river rises between the two, and near the place of rising pours into a vast region of fire, and forms a lake larger than the Mediterranean Sea, boiling with water and mud; and proceeding muddy and turbid, and winding about the earth, comes, among other places, to the extremities of the Acherusian Lake, but mingles not with the waters of the lake, and after making many coils about the earth plunges into Tartarus at a deeper level. This is that Pyriphlegethon, as the stream is called, which throws up jets of fire in all sorts of places. The fourth river goes out on the opposite side, and falls first of all into a wild and savage region, which is all of a dark-blue color, like lapis lazuli; and this is that river which is called the Stygian River, and falls into and forms the Lake Styx, and after falling into the lake and receiving strange powers in the waters, passes under the earth, winding round in the opposite direction to Pyriphlegethon, and meeting in the Acherusian Lake from the opposite side. And the water of this river too mingles with no other, but flows round in a circle and falls into Tartarus over against Pyriphlegethon, and the name of this river, as the poet says, is Cocytus.

Such is the name of the other world; and when the dead arrive at the place to which the genius of each severally conveys them, first of all they have sentence passed upon them, as they have lived well and piously or not. And those who appear to have lived neither well nor ill, go to the river Acheron, and mount such conveyances as they can get, and are carried in them to the lake, and there they dwell and are purified of their evil deeds, and suffer the penalty of the wrongs which they have done to others, and are absolved, and receive the rewards of their good deeds according to their deserts. But those who appear to be incurable by reason of the greatness of their crimes-who have committed many and terrible deeds of sacrilege, murders foul and violent, or the like-such are hurled into Tartarus, which is their suitable destiny, and they never come out. Those again who have committed crimes, which, although great, are not unpardonable-who in a moment of anger, for example, have done violence to a father or mother, and have repented for the remainder of their lives, or who have taken the life of another under like extenuating circumstances-these are plunged into Tartarus, the pains of which they are compelled to undergo for a year, but at the end of the year the wave casts them forth-mere homicides

by way of Cocytus, parricides and matricides by Pyriphlege-
thon-and they are borne to the Acherusian Lake, and there
they lift up their voices and call upon the victims whom they
have slain or wronged, to have pity on them, and to receive
them, and to let them come out of the river into the lake. And
if they prevail, then they come forth and cease from their
troubles; but if not, they are carried back again into Tartarus
and from thence into the rivers unceasingly, until they obtain mercy from those whom they have wronged: for that is
the sentence inflicted upon them by their judges. Those also
who are remarkable for having led holy lives are released
from this earthly prison, and go to their pure home which
is above, and dwell in the purer earth; and those who have
duly purified themselves with philosophy live henceforth altogether without the body, in mansions fairer far than these,
which may not be described, and of which the time would fail
me to tell.

Wherefore, Simmias, seeing all these things, what ought
not we to do in order to obtain virtue and wisdom in this life?
Fair is the prize, and the hope great.

I do not mean to affirm that the description which I
have given of the soul and her mansions is exactly true-a
man of sense ought hardly to say that. But I do say that, inasmuch as the soul is shown to be immortal, he may venture
to think, not improperly or unworthily, that something of the
kind is true. The venture is a glorious one, and he ought to
comfort himself with words like these, which is the reason
why lengthen out the tale. Wherefore, I say, let a man be of
good cheer about his soul, who has cast away the pleasures
and ornaments of the body as alien to him, and rather hurtful in their effects, and has followed after the pleasures of
knowledge in this life; who has adorned the soul in her own
proper jewels, which are temperance, and justice, and courage, and nobility, and truth-in these arrayed she is ready to
go on her journey to the world below, when her time comes.
You, Simmias and Cebes, and all other men, will depart at
some time or other. Me already, as the tragic poet would say,
the voice of fate calls. Soon I must drink the poison; and I

think that I had better repair to the bath first, in order that the women may not have the trouble of washing my body after I am dead.

When he had done speaking, Crito said: And have you any commands for us, Socrates-anything to say about your children, or any other matter in which we can serve you?

Nothing particular, he said: only, as I have always told you, I would have you look to yourselves; that is a service which you may always be doing to me and mine as well as to yourselves. And you need not make professions; for if you take no thought for yourselves, and walk not according to the precepts which I have given you, not now for the first time, the warmth of your professions will be of no avail.

We will do our best, said Crito. But in what way would you have us bury you?

In any way that you like; only you must get hold of me, and take care that I do not walk away from you. Then he turned to us, and added with a smile: I cannot make Crito believe that I am the same Socrates who have been talking and conducting the argument; he fancies that I am the other Socrates whom he will soon see, a dead body-and he asks, How shall he bury me? And though I have spoken many words in the endeavor to show that when I have drunk the poison I shall leave you and go to the joys of the blessed-these words of mine, with which I comforted you and myself, have had, I perceive, no effect upon Crito. And therefore I want you to be surety for me now, as he was surety for me at the trial: but let the promise be of another sort; for he was my surety to the judges that I would remain, but you must be my surety to him that I shall not remain, but go away and depart; and then he will suffer less at my death, and not be grieved when he sees my body being burned or buried. I would not have him sorrow at my hard lot, or say at the burial, Thus we lay out Socrates, or, Thus we follow him to the grave or bury him; for false words are not only evil in themselves, but they infect the soul with evil. Be of good cheer, then, my dear Crito, and say that you are burying my body only, and do with that as is usual, and as you think best.

When he had spoken these words, he arose and went into the bath chamber with Crito, who bade us wait; and we waited, talking and thinking of the subject of discourse, and also of the greatness of our sorrow; he was like a father of whom we were being bereaved, and we were about to pass the rest of our lives as orphans. When he had taken the bath his children were brought to him-(he had two young sons and an elder one); and the women of his family also came, and he talked to them and gave them a few directions in the presence of Crito; and he then dismissed them and returned to us.

Now the hour of sunset was near, for a good deal of time had passed while he was within. When he came out, he sat down with us again after his bath, but not much was said. Soon the jailer, who was the servant of the Eleven, entered and stood by him, saying: To you, Socrates, whom I know to be the noblest and gentlest and best of all who ever came to this place, I will not impute the angry feelings of other men, who rage and swear at me when, in obedience to the authorities, I bid them drink the poison-indeed, I am sure that you will not be angry with me; for others, as you are aware, and not I, are the guilty cause. And so fare you well, and try to bear lightly what must needs be; you know my errand. Then bursting into tears he turned away and went out.

Socrates looked at him and said: I return your good wishes, and will do as you bid. Then, turning to us, he said, How charming the man is: since I have been in prison he has always been coming to see me, and at times he would talk to me, and was as good as could be to me, and now see how generously he sorrows for me. But we must do as he says, Crito; let the cup be brought, if the poison is prepared: if not, let the attendant prepare some.

Yet, said Crito, the sun is still upon the hilltops, and many a one has taken the draught late, and after the announcement has been made to him, he has eaten and drunk, and indulged in sensual delights; do not hasten then, there is still time.

Socrates said: Yes, Crito, and they of whom you speak are right in doing thus, for they think that they will gain by the delay; but I am right in not doing thus, for I do not think that I should gain anything by drinking the poison a little later; I should be sparing and saving a life which is already gone: I could only laugh at myself for this. Please then to do as I say, and not to refuse me.

Crito, when he heard this, made a sign to the servant, and the servant went in, and remained for some time, and then returned with the jailer carrying a cup of poison. Socrates said: You, my good friend, who are experienced in these matters, shall give me directions how I am to proceed. The man answered: You have only to walk about until your legs are heavy, and then to lie down, and the poison will act. At the same time he handed the cup to Socrates, who in the easiest and gentlest manner, without the least fear or change of color or feature, looking at the man with all his eyes, Echecrates, as his manner was, took the cup and said: What do you say about making a libation out of this cup to any god? May I, or not? The man answered: We only prepare, Socrates, just so much as we deem enough. I understand, he said: yet I may and must pray to the gods to prosper my journey from this to that other world-may this, then, which is my prayer, be granted to me. Then holding the cup to his lips, quite readily and cheerfully he drank off the poison. And hitherto most of us had been able to control our sorrow; but now when we saw him drinking, and saw too that he had finished the draught, we could no longer forbear, and in spite of myself my own tears were flowing fast; so that I covered my face and wept over myself, for certainly I was not weeping over him, but at the thought of my own calamity in having lost such a companion. Nor was I the first, for Crito, when he found himself unable to restrain his tears, had got up and moved away, and I followed; and at that moment. Apollodorus, who had been weeping all the time, broke out in a loud cry which made cowards of us all. Socrates alone retained his calmness: What is this strange outcry? he said. I sent away the women mainly in order that they might not offend in this way, for I have heard that a man should die in peace. Be quiet, then, and have patience.

When we heard that, we were ashamed, and refrained our tears; and he walked about until, as he said, his legs began to fail, and then he lay on his back, according to the directions, and the man who gave him the poison now and then looked at his feet and legs; and after a while he pressed his foot hard and asked him if he could feel; and he said, no; and then his leg, and so upwards and upwards, and showed us that he was cold and stiff. And he felt them himself, and said: When the poison reaches the heart, that will be the end. He was beginning to grow cold about the groin, when he uncovered his face, for he had covered himself up, and said (they were his last words)-he said: Crito, I owe a cock to Asclepius; will you remember to pay the debt? The debt shall be paid, said Crito; is there anything else? There was no answer to this question; but in a minute or two a movement was heard, and the attendants uncovered him; his eyes were set, and Crito closed his eyes and mouth.

Such was the end, Echecrates, of our friend, whom I may truly call the wisest, and justest, and best of all the men whom I have ever known.

-THE END-

CPSIA information can be obtained
at www.ICGtesting.com
Printed in the USA
BVHW030218160722
642304BV00008B/143

9 781537 061740